Con

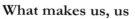

Preface – In memory of Tony and Richard

I simply could not believe it.

One of my running buddies, Tony, had taken his own life.

The cheeky chappie, who was always so happy to help and motivate others, to make them smile, to have a laugh and a joke, was no longer with us.

My friends and I had no idea that there were any issues, that he may have been depressed or had suicidal thoughts. We only found out when it was too late. We will never know what was going through his head in the days/weeks/months leading up to his death. What was he worried about? What was preying on his mind? Was he concerned about his future? Was he in turmoil about his current situation? We simply do not know why he thought enough is enough, and he decided to take his own life.

Unfortunately, this is not an isolated incident, nor has it been for many years. Male suicide is still the biggest killer of men under 40 in the UK and the second biggest in the USA.

My work colleague and friend Richard has recently taken his own life, a young lad in his 30s with a wife and two young kids. Again, why did this happen? Why didn't he talk to someone? Why didn't he reach out to a friend for help? I know he was struggling a little, but I never thought he was struggling so much that he only saw one solution. I always made a point in asking how he was doing, but now I think, what more could I have done to help? I cannot comprehend how his young family and parents are dealing with this right now and how they will deal with this moving forward.

Tony and Richard were just two of many young men who made the devastating decision to end their lives. If only we had known what

they had been going through. That their friends and family would have been there to talk through whatever issues they had, to reassure them that things would get better and maybe things weren't as bad as they seemed. To have been able to give them the hope and confidence that life is worth living after all.

The pain, heartache, and guilt of those nearest and dearest to them are the ones that suffer for many, many years after their loved one has passed away.

So why is this such a horrifically common occurrence? Is it simply that us blokes don't feel we can talk openly and honestly about our troubles and fears with others? Is it deep routed from our childhood that we must "man up" and get on with it? To not show any perceived weakness or fragility, is that what must be maintained at all costs?

I refuse to sit by and do nothing as yet another bloke gets so down and depressed with life that they see suicide as the only option. That they feel nobody wants to know how they are feeling, that the world would be better off without them. When nothing could be further from the truth.

I have seen first-hand the devastation that suicide leaves behind. I cannot, and will not, sit around playing on my PlayStation when I could be doing something a lot more productive and very much needed, i.e., helping as many blokes as I can to stay alive.

This is why I have felt compelled to write this book.

One suicide is one too many.

Us blokes can doubt ourselves and our capabilities. I have been there. I have bought, worn and washed the proverbial t-shirt. It is entirely normal when we think we are not good enough when we are criticised or mocked. It is how we deal with this external negative opinion and the subsequent internal doubting monologue which is crucial to our state of mind.

I am one of the lucky ones. I can now share my thoughts and fears with several close mates without fear of ridicule or embarrassment. I have fantastic friends who are always willing to listen whenever I need them. They also know I will always be there for them too.

Throughout this book, I will share some trials and tribulations from my past, my neuroses, lack of confidence, feelings of low self-worth, and how I have come out the other side to finally feel content in my own skin and at peace with myself. I still have days when I struggle to remain positive but I know that whatever is bothering me will be temporary.

I will focus on the pivotal stages of our lives and put forward ideas that can help you deal with the all too possible challenging events that will befall you throughout your life.

To help show you that there is always a silver lining in a sky full of clouds, to give hope that there is a life out there waiting to be enjoyed, not just endured.

If this book can help just one bloke stop and think, to realise that they can make things better for themselves and those around them or enable them to reach out and ask for help, it will have been worth it.

This is me

I would just like to tell you a little about me:

- I am a simple, straightforward bloke.
- I am not an expert in life,
- I am definitely not perfect. Nobody is.
- I do my best, that's good enough
- If you don't like me, that's not my problem
- I take a positive outlook on life and love to make people smile with my general silliness.
- I don't take myself too seriously(see above).
- I want to make a positive difference to those around me
- My writing skills are distinctly average(see below).

This book is not a miracle cure for unhappiness and despair. You will not magically become a happier person by simply reading this book. But what I hope it can do is help you realise you can change your life for the better and become more optimistic, less stressed and more at ease with yourself.

But to make change happen, you really need to want to change. If you know you need to but don't actually want to, you simply won't change.

Hoping life will change for the better rarely, if ever, works out. Whingeing about life will definitely not make it better. Getting off your arse and actually doing what you need to improve your life is the way forward.

Not everything in this book will resonate with you, but I hope enough of it will help you believe in yourself and start enjoying life again.

How are you feeling about your life at the moment?

Are you happy and content with the way your life is going at the minute? Do you have a job you enjoy doing? Do you and your other half still want to spend time with each other? I guess the answer to at least one of these questions may be a no, along with most of the male population, but I hope it's a yes to all 3, and if so, keep up the good work.

Everyone gets stuck in a rut after a while, doing the same things, going to the same places. Whilst this can be comforting, it can become frustrating and really rather dull.

It usually takes us until our forties to realise we could be doing something more with our lives, which thankfully still gives us time to start experiencing more, achieving more, and becoming more fulfilled.

But as we grow older, our ability to take on new ideas, to try out new ways of doing things, becomes much more difficult as we become more and more set in our ways. Therefore, the sooner we wake up and "smell the coffee", the better. Our habits become so ingrained, we can't, or don't, want to change them.

While our school years and teenage years can be stressful and troubling, I am sure the years between the twenties and fifties are the most challenging ones. We have so many responsibilities and decisions to make that it can get overwhelming.

In some parts of our lives, we can keep some semblance of control. We decide what to eat, what to do in our spare time, in others, not so much, i.e., when a loved one suddenly dies.

But it's how we manage to deal with the day-to-day challenges that can make us or break us.

There are usually three ways we deal with challenges:

- We ignore or avoid them at all costs; we mentally or physically run away.
- We take them personally and beat ourselves up about them repeatedly.
- We embrace them and take them as learning experiences to improve how we deal with future challenges.

I was definitely in the middle group until my early 30s; I wasted so much time and energy stressing about bugger all.

It's the last choice that is the most difficult to do but also the most fulfilling. Accepting the challenge and learning from it is definitely the way forward.

There is always a choice of how we react, even if it doesn't feel like it. Most of the time, we don't think, we just react. But we don't have to scream and shout at everything and everyone, blaming God, the world, the missus, the boss, for whatever has kicked us in the bollocks.

It is down to us. It's our decision. We get to choose how we deal with the situation.

We can be that guy that flies off the handle at the tiniest little thing, or we can take a deep breath, think for a second, then realise it's not worth getting worked up about.

This is sometimes easier said than done, but we need to work at it to remain sane. If we don't, it becomes the proverbial vicious circle; we get more and more wound up until we lose it big time or have a complete meltdown.

We can also be guilty of reading too much into certain situations, overthinking, then over-reacting, then getting annoyed because something didn't go the way we thought it should or how we wanted it to go.

It's not the world around us getting us down. We manage that far too well on our own.

It's also important to focus on how you can make the most out of each and every day, not rue the days before, or worry about the days ahead. The old adage of taking one day at a time is most definitely a sound one.

Why? I hear you ask! Honest, I did. You can't change the past. You can't predict the future, so don't worry about it or dwell on it either!

Just try and enjoy each day, one day at a time. If you have a bad day, so what, shit happens, tomorrow is a new day, a clean slate.

Having a bad day and getting through it without losing your shit means you are learning and winning the daily game of life.

With hindsight (that wonderful elusive bugger), I would have written this at least ten years ago, but I wasn't quite there yet. Now (at the age of 48 at the time of writing), I am at a stage in life where I am finally confident in my own skin. I have finally accepted I am who I am and that my best is more than good enough.

I really want to make a positive difference to the world (a bit grand, I know) by helping as many blokes as possible to deal with the stresses and strains in everyday life.

Throughout the numerous chapters of this book, I will ask you to make a choice, a commitment to yourself, to what you intend to do moving forward. I have made it nice and straightforward.

You can either:

Enjoy: The **HITS**   -   Happiness In Thy Self

                         Or

End up with: The **SHITS**   -   Suffer Hopelessly In
                                               The Shit

You always have a choice, to make the best of life and strive for the HITS or do nothing, become more unhappy, day by day, and end up with, the SHITS, forever.

Also, throughout this book will be a smattering of little Tips

The **TIPS**   -   Top Info produces Success

These are there for you to try out, and they will hopefully put you on the track to a happier, less frustrated life.

This is your life
(make sure you live it)

We can think of our lives as just one big story. It has a beginning, a middle, and an end.

We have a cast of the usual protagonists/situations.

- The lead character (you)
- The baddie/s
- The love interest/s
- The significant other/s
- The femme/male Fatale
- The friends
- The enemies
- The calamitous occurrence or 7
- The death of a loved one
- The helpful strangers
- The horrible bosses
- The loyal pets
- The family
- The happy ending (hopefully)
- The cliff-hanger
- The final scene

This may sound like a movie cast, but that's no surprise; where do you think most directors draw some of their thoughts and ideas from? Their own life experiences.

There will be several significant events throughout our lifetime:

- Births
- Deaths
- Marriage
- Breakups
- Divorce
- Having kids
- Losing a job
- Epic nights out
- Terrible nights out
- Epic holidays
- Terrible holidays

Imagine a filmmaker recording everything from your life last year and made a movie from it. Please answer the following questions truthfully, don't lie to yourself.

1) Would you be proud of it?
2) Would you be embarrassed?
3) Would you be shocked?
4) Would you be angry?
5) Would you be sad and miserable?
6) Would you say you did your best?

If you answered yes to questions 1 & 6, but no to everything else, you must be having a pretty good life, well done! Keep doing what you are doing!

If you answered no to questions 1 and/or 6 and yes to at least a few of the remaining questions, you need to take a big deep breath and look at what makes you miserable and do something about it.

We have a finite amount of time on this earth, and unfortunately, or fortunately, we don't know exactly for how long. So this is why I will continually implore you to make the most of each and every day.

Many factors can affect your time on this earth:

- **Your Health – Mental and Physical**
- **Your job – Physically demanding and/or mentally stressful?**
- **Your home life**
- **Your Diet**
- **Your habits**
- **The amount of exercise you do**
- **The people you hang around with**
- *Luck*
- How you deal with Life-changing events
- Extreme weather
- Other External factors

Some of the above are **in your control**, others are not, and we spend far too much time stressing about what we can't control, which is not only distressing but absolutely pointless.

By concentrating on the ones **within your control** (i.e., most of them), you can make dealing with the uncontrollable ones much more manageable.

Life doesn't have to be a ball ache. By buying this book (and hopefully actually reading it), you have decided to start looking into how you can get more out of your life and that you are tired of the same old, same old routine.

But knowing you should do something about it isn't enough. You need to want to change. Reset your mindset, behaviour, habits and attitude because if you don't want it enough, it simply won't happen. Believe in yourself, that you can become the ideal version of yourself. Let's crack on, you can do this.

What makes us, us?

This chapter looks back in time to reflect and understand why we are the way we are.

Whilst we can't change the past, it makes sense to understand what we have learned from our life up until this point. If you can do this, you can increase your chances of having a much more meaningful and happier life.

The Beginning

I shall start by stating the obvious, you can't choose your parents. Until you are squeezed or cut out into this world, you are entirely oblivious to your impending life before you. Your first thought is probably WTF *it's bright and cold here, can I go back, please?*

Once you are over the initial shock, it's all about the basics, all very primaeval – we need food, warmth and lots of cuddles. One of the first experiences of discomfort probably comes from sitting in a pile of our own shit, not the most pleasant I can imagine, even if I can't remember this. However, I do remember the horrifying moment in secondary school when a little bit of poo came out with a fart, oh how I laughed, not.

We learn very early in life that screaming our lungs out means we get some attention. Our parents have to work out what the hell we are crying about - do we need food? Are we cold? Have we soiled ourselves yet again?

The first few years fly by for us, or I assume so, as I can't remember much before my 4th birthday. Our parents will undoubtedly remember the sleepless nights, the colic, diarrhea, much puking, and many other challenging childhood maladies. But then there's the flip side to the anxiety and stress, the joy of seeing your child smile when they recognise your voice and look around to see you. To hear them giggle helplessly at Gerry the giraffe who has just appeared as if by magic, then again 4 seconds later as if it is a brand new experience.

As parents, it's so important how we deal with our little ones in those early years. It makes a massive difference to the rest of their lives. Initial insecurities can be formed by our parents' behavior and their actions. However, most parents only think about getting more than 3 hours of sleep a day and staying sane.

I shall state it again, we can't choose our parents, but we can choose not to follow their bad habits, but I appreciate not at 4 years old. Most of the time we are completely oblivious that we have organically taken them on anyway, no matter how hard we try not to. Self-awareness doesn't come to us unless we start looking at how we conduct ourselves on a daily basis. There isn't anyone around us at the age of 10 to tell us that our parents hitting each other is not great and not normal behavior. If it becomes a regular occurrence for us, then guess what? We think hitting other people is normal. Yup, Well fucked up.

This leads to the whole nature vs nurture debate. Some say one is more prevalent than the other. I, and many others, believe it's a mixture of the two, but the environment we are brought up in also significantly impacts.

Nature

Nature is our DNA, yup, back to our parents again. We hit the ground running with some of Mummy and Daddies dodgy chromosomes and hope to get some of the good ones too. At this stage, we are the stereotypical blank page, ready to get the pen out and start writing.

We act as the proverbial sponge in our early years, sucking up any information we get, holding it tight. The first five years of our lives form the basis of what type of adult we grow into. Some deep-rooted habits and fears are born from this early age. Thankfully other factors also influence. Some make things better, others make things worse, but we typically don't notice until it's too late. The sooner the moment of reflection upon the "why" we do the things we do, the better. Please don't wait till your forties like me!

We should allow ourselves to believe and trust that there could be a much better way of doing things, which will probably be far better for you as an individual and those around you.

So, this is a very brief and basic overview of nature. It is the foundation of our lives, the beginning of what makes us, us. It's how we build on that foundation which makes such a pivotal difference to our lives in the future. This is where the nurture bit comes into play.

Nurture

How we are brought up makes a massive difference in what type of adult we turn into. If our parents are loving and very polite, we will likely take on these traits. If your parents are lazy, uncouth, and don't give a shit about themselves, the environment or anything in particular, then I am afraid you may well pick up some of these traits. But always remember you are not your parents, you are you, and you have the choice to be who you are.

So, this is my story:

My parents were (and still are) lovely, well-meaning and decent people. They both had pretty tough childhoods. My mum was the oldest of 8 kids and spent much of her childhood helping her parents bring up her little brothers and sisters, with very little 'me time' or playing out with friends. My Dad had a pretty tough time too. He lost both his brother and father before his 20's. These moments shaped how my parents brought up my brother and I. I was the oldest by about 4 years and, being the first child, was the one they practiced being parents on. Luckily, this mostly went ok. However, my mother's maternal instincts kicked in at nursery. I hated it and made a massive fuss. In fact, I cried so much my mum thought it best to keep me at home until I started school. This well-meaning act of kindness backfired because I wasn't ready for it when I started proper school - cue more crying and distress.

It took a couple of years to finally snap myself out of this, with a little bit of help from Dad. Before I divulge the next bit, I am actually grateful for what happened as it sorted me out, and I finally started to kind of enjoy going to school. My Dad, who'd had enough of my crying, gave my arse a smack, which shocked me, but it worked. I know he felt guilty for doing it as he never did it again, and whilst we see this as unacceptable now, I am glad it happened as it stopped me from being a really soft little shit. I was now just a little soft shit.

The rest of primary school passed without too much further distress and occasionally some fun. We were lucky enough to have a decently sized playground and field at school, cue lots of running-based games.

It's funny what you remember from your formative years. I remember gagging at the smell and taste of warm milk in the summer. I remember a Christmas play where I was one of the 3 kings (I was pretty chuffed with that one). I remember a kind and caring teacher, Mrs. Roper. I remember a rather unpleasant teacher, Mrs. R. I also remember the slightly scary headteacher, a nun called Sister M.A. I never saw her smile once. I remember being sent to her because I was flicking crumbs at the dinner table. This apparently deserved a beating with a slipper. I never did flick another crumb though, lesson learnt.

I also remember my first utterance of a swear word. I was getting my coat on in the cloakroom and managed to hurt myself on one of the wooden benches, to which I said, "*Aaaaaa, you bugger*", cue every kid around me shouting, "we're going to tell on you"!

Quite funny really, when 2 years later, at middle school, they were all telling each other to fuck off.

Moving on to Middle school, we had a right couple of characters as teachers, a French teacher who had a bit of a temper and liked to throw blackboard rubbers at you if you misbehaved, a slightly scary PE teacher. Still, we knew where we stood. If we messed around, there were consequences, and we soon learned not to piss around too much.

Today, teachers have a rather tough gig with very little authority. The pendulum has swung too far the other way now, with parents having a right go at teachers for telling off little Johnny, who is a proper little shit, but is the apple of mummy's eye. There seems to be a lot less respect for teachers, and they struggle to command authority without the fear of losing their job or being sued.

Teachers have an enormous responsibility as they can make a massive difference to what type of adult we grow into. Not only do they have the capability to teach us about the usual school subjects, but they can also teach us how to learn and take feedback.

With the correct amount of encouragement and praise and given in the right manner and context, this can make a real difference in the development of a young person's life and self-worth. A bad teacher can make you hate learning and school. A brilliant one can help you see what can be achieved with hard work.

I hear people refer to their time in school as some of the best years of their lives. I wish I could say the same, but that would be complete bollocks. There are very valid reasons for this. School life for me, up until the age of 16, was a somewhat fraught and stressful time....

School Life & Teenage tribulations

Wow, where do I start!

As lads, we all hope puberty comes to us as soon as possible so that we can start the journey from boy to man. This rarely goes smoothly.

Until the age of 9 or 10, girls weren't even on the radar. I was too busy playing British bulldog and riding around on my bike to even think about them. Then breasts started emerging, and girls suddenly appeared on my radar, and so began my fitful and mostly fruitless attempts at getting a girlfriend. The fact that I didn't know how to be cool in front of girls (or in general) or be confident in any shape or form probably didn't help.

The fact I was also relatively short for my age probably didn't help either, as you can see in the below picture of me with my schoolmates in a footy shot when I was 11 - guess which one I am!

I was thrilled we only had 12 full strips, not. This did not help my already fragile confidence levels.

I certainly wasn't part of the cool kid's gang. I just didn't have the confidence. I was pretty afraid and unsure of virtually everything. Thankfully I had a small group of friends I could trust, which worked out pretty well.

I really wish I could have been able to relax and chill out, not fret, not worry, not give a shit what people thought of me. To have been content and confident in myself would have been epic.

It is difficult to engage with the opposite sex when you feel very self-conscious about yourself. That's probably why I did so badly with the ladies. I could barely say hello, never mind "chat them up" the only time I managed to relax and be myself was on a trip to Ford castle with a completely different group of people from another school as part of their school band. I could just be myself, and they just accepted me for who I was, and I relaxed and enjoyed myself.

As I headed into high school, things were turned up a couple of notches, I was bullied by several lovely individuals. Sorry, I mean twats.

I don't understand why this happens. Why do some kids see a scared, nervous kid then decide to make that kid's life worse by making fun of them, making it their mission to hurt and upset them? Is it to make themselves feel better about themselves? Seriously? WTF. Do they think they have to have that power over others? Do they want to be the confident big shot? Are they so insecure they have to prove they are not, by showing how fucking "tough" they are? Yeah, really tough picking on the small, insecure kid. Well done, wankers.

Bullying can ruin lives, and if not addressed and sorted, can have long-lasting negative implications.

When someone repeatedly calls you a soft little shit, it's hard not to start believing it. You begin to worry all the time, start doubting everything you do.

When you are a 13-year-old kid, it's hard not to take it to heart and just ignore the arseholes.

It might actually be worse today as there is no respite from the Instagram comments and Facebook, nor do the schools handle bullying in a timely manner.

Another reason for bullying is the bullies may feel threatened by another's good looks (this one didn't apply to me!) or intelligence (nor this one), and they work to put others down and humiliate them so that they feel better or less shit about themselves.

Unfortunately, there are far too many teenage suicides caused by the constant barrage of hate towards them, just for being naturally pretty or brainy. Thankfully I had several decent mates that made school just about bearable, and as time went by, the bullies got a bit bored and finally left me alone. Most of them left at 16 and didn't go to 6th form, which worked well for me.

So, what's the moral of this section? Apart from don't let the bastards get you down?

From a parental perspective, I would always keep a close lookout for your child's moods and behaviours around school. Are they faking sickness so they don't have to go in? Ask them if they are being bullied and help them with some coping mechanisms, like a baseball bat, only joking, mostly. Seriously, the best thing to do with bullies is not to react, ignore them, don't let them get to you. Impress upon your child that they can get through it and reiterate that if you can stand up to them and hide your fear, they will hopefully leave you alone.

If it gets really bad, make sure you approach the school, they have a duty of care for their students and should give a shit about their health and wellbeing, rather than turning a blind eye.

Then work on increasing your child's self-esteem, praising them, helping them believe in themselves, and try to get them to realise that other peoples' opinions are just that, opinions.

Early Adult life

When we reach 16, we have a few decisions to make, and it depends a lot on how the last 3 years at school have gone. Getting decent grades gives you more choice on where your next step could be.

It's time to decide whether to continue education or start working and earning some money.

Some people always plan on going to Uni. Others really don't want to. It's all down to personal preference. There is no right or wrong, only what is right at that moment.

Yes, you may regret your decision, but either way, at least you made a decision. That's the main thing.

Here's my story:

I was a distinctly average student. I did just enough to get into 6th form to do three A-levels, Maths, Physics and Chemistry. I didn't know what I wanted to do long term, the career advice was a bit pants, but I realised if I passed my chosen A-levels to a half-decent standard, I could do lots of different degrees at Uni. I went down the Uni route as I wasn't confident enough to go and find a proper job, and I was also told that I could go into work at a higher level and wage bracket with a degree.

In the end, I just got good enough grades to do an Electrical and Electronic Engineering degree at the University of Northumbria at Newcastle, which was Newcastle Poly for the first year (just saying). I did look at Huddersfield and

Nottingham, but in the end, I took the easy option (and the cheapest) by going to Newcastle. I just commuted to and from home each day. Back in the day, I was lucky enough to have my course fees paid for by the government, and I also got a small grant.

Uni was pretty good fun, real-life was yet to kick in. It was just a bit of coursework then partying with friends. The 3rd year of my course was a year out in industry. It was almost like a proper job, but with shit pay. This gave me my first taste of office politics, how certain people really didn't like each other and how they begrudgingly got on with each other (mostly) to get the job done, eventually.

Looking back on this time, I can recognise that a lot of the friction was due to their egos. If they actually accepted each other for their good and bad points, that they could have differing points of view, then they could have been much more productive and maybe, just maybe, enjoyed coming to work.

Likeminded people get on with each other. Those with different viewpoints, values and habits can get on each other's nerves. It's far better to have a growth mindset and learn to appreciate each other's point of view rather than whingeing their tits off about them all day long.

After a year in industry, it was back to Uni for the final year. I scraped through my exams, then started looking for a job. After a couple of weeks and a few interviews, I was lucky enough to be offered a role in a small electronics firm only 2 miles from my front door. There were certainly pros and cons to this.

The pro was I could get to and from home pretty quickly (4 minutes in a car). The con was I was the closest employee to the office, so I was given the responsibility for opening and closing the factory. I was also the first responder for the alarm system. I had many early morning calls saying the alarm has gone off, but thankfully almost all were false alarms, a pesky spider or bird were usually the culprit.

This first proper job was a rite of passage.

I worked at a local Manufacturing firm in the town where I lived. My first role was as Production Manager. This was my primary role, but since it was a small company, I ended up doing loads of secondary jobs: PCB designer, test engineer, product tester, site support, fault finder, and also helping out on the production line with the lads and lasses.

The production line work was a great way of learning about the product and my colleagues. It gave me some great insight into what works and what doesn't when managing people, i.e., leading by example and being firm but fair and, above all, even-handed!

When I first joined, there were only 4 production staff, and unsurprisingly they were all very different. There was the laid-back jack the lad, the angry one, the eccentric one and the amenable one. Those first couple of years were tough, trying to get the lads working as efficiently as possible, but it was an excellent learning opportunity ref people management! This is the polite and positive way of putting it. It was an absolute fucking nightmare a lot of the time, but I got on with it and survived, thankfully.

There were 3 joint owners of the company, the old pipe-smoking MD, the characterful technical Director, and the Finance Director. This last individual was to become the source of many different emotions over my time at the company.

I learned so much in those first 10 years. It was rather stressful at times, but there were also some fun times. As time went on, we took on more staff, moved to bigger premises, expanded the portfolio. Our little company went from strength to strength.

Sometimes we worked silly hours to get a job out of the door, but it was really rather satisfying completing an order to a tight deadline.

As a young bloke, I was somewhat naive and still doubted my abilities quite a lot, but I always worked hard and tried my best, and thankfully I got rewarded for this in the form of regular pay increases and bonuses. However, as the company grew, so did the pressure and stress, working long hours and dealing with more staff. I also spent a lot of my time stressing over things I couldn't control, like other people's behaviour....

I didn't realise that it's not good to always try and please others, as it will never be enough, no matter how hard you try. It just ends up with you feeling like shit when they put you down for not being able to read their mind, or they change their mind halfway through. Or they just want to wind you up and see you squirm, to prove they know more than you, and put you down.

So, let's get back to the Financial Director, who also took care of operations and was my direct line manager.

It started off pretty well, he would encourage me, support me and reward me. If I messed up, he would berate me, but that was fair enough. I even kind of liked him and looked up to him.

But as time went by, I think the strain of running a larger company took some toll on him. He started to turn into a rather nasty bully. He also got a lot more arrogant, thinking he could do whatever he wanted because he was the company's owner. One of the main issues was that he was so inconsistent at times, praising you for good work, telling you not to worry about a small mistake, then other times he just lost the plot and had a massive go over something small and inconsequential. One that sticks in mind was when I was highlighting a slight increase in price from our painting supplier for a particular colour. He went mental, calling the supplier and me all sorts, even though we were charging the customer more for the special colour, which more than made up for the slight increase. He must have been having a bad day, which tipped him over the edge, but there was worse to come.

I had been working for the company for about 10 years by this point, and this individual had now been such a shit that he had given one guy a nervous breakdown and maltreated a couple of others, so much so that they left the company. He was actually getting worse.

The tipping point for me was an incident involving my laptop bag. I had recently won a driving experience with Nissan, and they had given us a load of goodies at the end of the day. One of which was a decent Laptop bag.

Now, one day I left this bag in the FD's office, thought nothing of it, I forgot that I had left it in there, to be honest, then realised I had misplaced it. After looking for it for several days, I finally spotted the FD using it! So I respectfully asked for it back "yeah, yeah, no problem, I'll give it to you tomorrow" was the answer. Anyway, this went on for several days, even a couple of weeks. Finally, I had had enough. One night when I was the last one in the office, I noticed he had left my bag in his office as I was dropping off a report. So, after humming and hawing over whether I should take it back, I did just that. I removed his paperwork from my bag and neatly placed it on his desk where he could see it.

I then took my bag, locked up and headed home.

So, the next day I was doing my usual routine of setting the lads their daily workload when he came storming into the Production area, all angry and red-faced and told me to get into his office, which I did.

He really went for it this time, how dare I take the bag, he was using it etc. etc., and I tried to calmly say I had asked for it numerous times and you hadn't given it to me, so I took it back. It then went up another level with him effing and jeffing. He actually called me a Fxcking Cxnt. To say I was rather shocked would be an understatement. This was the beginning of the end for any respect I had for the guy, and I actually started to hate him, which grew over time.

Thankfully he finally got his comeuppance when another colleague lodged an official complaint with our owners in Canada, and I was called in to give any examples of when he mistreated me. I simply recounted the story above.

This was the beginning of the end for him. After several meetings, he left the business, he wasn't sacked as such, but they were generous to him, even though he didn't really deserve it.

The only good thing to come of my time under the FD was it did toughen me up. I became more resilient. But it was a close thing, he nearly broke me. Thankfully I had some excellent friends in the company that I could talk to, which helped massively. Thank you, Terry, Terry & Steve.

After this, life at the company got a lot better, we got a new boss who was lovely, but unfortunately, he was a little too nice and a little indecisive. However, he supported me and helped me massively by putting me on a "brilliant" personal development course, which I will cover in the self-confidence chapter.

After approx. 10 years after the FD "left," I finally made my peace with him. After several years of hating him, I finally realised that there was no point in holding a grudge. Life is too short, so I shook his hand at a trade show and said, let bygones be bygones. I still see him from time to time, and I think he has mellowed. I hope he has become happier with himself and isn't such a shit to others anymore.

So, what have did I learn through these early work experiences?

The **TIPS**

- Don't take everything personally
- Opinion is only that, nothing more.
- Consistency is key
- Hard work can be satisfying
- Doing your best is good enough
- Admit it when you are wrong
- Be open to other people's suggestions
- Give clear instructions, reiterate, ask for confirmation
- Always give praise to a job well done
- Use a shit sandwich when you need to tell someone off: positive – negative -positive

Relationships

Always a tricky one this one.

As humans, we crave companionship. Most of us want or need friends. We usually develop a desire to find a close permanent companion. Someone to love, that someone special who you want to be with all the time, and maybe start a family, to keep this little thing called the human race going.

Finding that perfect "one" can either be very exciting or a somewhat convoluted and stressful process, usually a mixture of both. A series of trial-and-error attempts to find and create a fulfilling relationship can be rather fraught, but sometimes we are lucky and find someone fun to be around, other times not so much.

The thing is, if you don't try, you will never know. Most of us are filled with doubt and are fearful of getting hurt or rejected, this sometimes stops us even trying. When we have been broken and shat on from above, it makes us very wary about opening ourselves up to another person in case the same thing happens again.

It is rather difficult for some people to pluck up the courage to talk to someone they like the look of, never mind "chat them up". I was definitely one of these people. I never really had enough confidence to just start chatting to some random lass that I liked the look of when out on a night out with my mates, never mind asking them if they would like to meet up for a date at a later date.

The only reason I started talking to my now wife in a Newcastle nightclub many, many years ago was because of my mate Chris. It was a typical Friday night in town, and it was towards the end of the evening. Despite our drunken stupor, he noticed this very pretty lass with curly hair smiling at me.

Then out of the blue, and out of character (he was just as bad as me at chatting up the ladies), he drunkenly swayed across the dancefloor to tell her I fancied her, which gave me the kick up the arse I needed to go over and introduce myself.

The rest, as they say, is history.

At the beginning of any relationship, we start by getting to know the other person. Finding out what they like, what they enjoy doing, what past experiences they have had, what their hopes and dreams are. We have a raft of emotions, from excitement to worry and doubt. But hopefully, happiness and, at some point, maybe even love.

We need to let the other person know about ourselves, our authentic selves, not the made-up fake ones on Facebook. For any relationship to last, you need to be honest with yourself and your partner; otherwise, it's somewhat doomed for failure. Because eventually, the effort from trying to be someone else all the time will grind you down. Then, when the other person realises you have been lying to them all this time, this will sour the relationship, probably ending in a breakup.

Relationships need constant effort because life is not perfect. It sometimes has blood, sweat and tears. It's not all love and happiness.

If you say you have the perfect happy relationship, you are probably lying or delusional.

I have been married for over 20 years, we have 2 great kids, a dog, a half-decent house, and we manage to have a holiday most years. I am rather fortunate.

Yes, my wife and I get on each other's tits occasionally, and we can argue about stupid little things like virtually every couple on the planet, but on the whole, we get on pretty damn well.

I still love her to bits, which helps.

The longer we stay together as a couple or husband and wife, the more we can take each other for granted. We tend not to make as much of an effort that we used to do. We get lazy, get stuck doing the same things day in and day out. We need to continue making an effort, keep talking to each other, continue doing nice things for each other, and above all, respect one another. Not shout or take offence when our partner calls us out about something we have done. Don't let your ego get in the way, and get very defensive, then have a go at them, as it will only turn into a massive argument, usually over nothing.

I think the phrase don't sweat the small stuff really is one saying we need to take heed of. But one person's small stuff might mean a massive deal to the other. For instance, a guy makes his lunch and leaves a few crumbs on the worktop. Not an enormous deal, unless your wife has spent the whole morning cleaning the kitchen and has put a lot of time and effort into making everything clean and tidy, then it's a massive deal to her. So, you probably know what she's like, just spend the 4 seconds wiping the work surface down before you leave the kitchen.

Blokes look at things in much simpler terms. We tend not to overthink or overcomplicate things too much. Our lovely ladies, however, think about everything.

I think it all comes down to respect and acceptance. If you respect your partner's point of view, the way they do things, accept that they do things differently and think differently, then you will have a lot fewer arguments over pointless shit. You will have a much more relaxed relationship. You may even enjoy it!

In the end, it's all about balance, compromise, and compassion.

Happy wife, happy life.

Choice time

The **HITS**

Make an effort, keep talking, be caring and supportive, have a fulfilling, happy relationship.

or

The **SHITS**

Be selfish, get angry, stop communicating, destroy your relationship, get a messy divorce and have financial issues.

Parenthood

So, you finally meet someone you can see yourself spending the rest of your life with, you may decide to get married and/or choose to have a kid, or it may happen by accident. Whichever way it happens nine months later (God willing), your partner will have a little baby, or if things don't happen naturally, you may adopt your little bundle of joy.

After the exciting initial act of creating a little one, everything starts to change on so many levels. Your relationship will begin to change. You will start planning what colour to paint the "baby bedroom" rather than which resort in Ibiza to go to. Then you start buying loads of baby paraphernalia, from baby clothes to prams, sterilisers, baby bottles, and nappies, lots of nappies. No more new bikes, cars, or designer jeans, not unless you want to start arguing already. It's about resetting your expectations and accept that things will change. If you resist and try and do the same things you have always done, you will start resenting it when you can't do them.

As blokes, we really can't comprehend the changes our partner goes through while pregnant, the morning sickness, the body shape change, the cravings, the tiredness, the mood swings. All you can do is ride the wave. Just be there to support and sympathise, oh, and maybe reduce your alcohol consumption as your pregnant partner can't drink, try not to rub this in!

I would definitely get as much sleep as possible during pregnancy because after the birth…

It's certainly a bit of shock to the system this one. You get all excited for your little one's birth, then realise it's bloody hard work: Sleepless nights, crying, stinky, dirty nappies and vomit, all good stuff. With bugger all sleep, both parents get rather ratty and irritable, the trick here is to work together to allow one to have some rest time whilst the other, quite literally, holds the baby.

I remember when my eldest daughter was born, the birth was somewhat fraught, with my poor missus having a 40-hour labour, then there was cutting and forceps, really rather scary, but thankfully mother and baby were fine, and within 48 hours, they both safely home.

Every time I picked her up for the first few weeks, I was afraid of doing something wrong, not holding her correctly, dropping her, it was really rather stressful. But gradually, I got used to her and really started to enjoy being a dad. My wife took to it like a duck to water, a born mother, she did an epic job with both of our daughters, and she still does.

When those first few smiles arrive, the giggles make all the hard work worthwhile. Watching your baby giggle at something you do is such an epic feeling.

Before you know it, teeth start arriving and teething begins, bright red cheeks, much crying. Then they start trying to speak, become mobile, crawling, then walking, you really have to have your wits about you, one minute they are right beside you then they disappear. It's all part of the parenthood experience.

Once they eventually start sleeping through the night, this brings some normality and routine back into your life. When you start taking them places, you realise just how much crap you have to take with you; bottles, food, nappies, wet wipes, Sudocrem, pushchair, spare clothes and blankets. Taking a kid under the age of 2 abroad is, frankly, hard work, and unless you holiday with a set of parents, you will probably come back even more tired. Mind you, even then it depends on whether you get on with your parents!

Before you know it, they will be starting nursery, then into first school. Where the real fun begins for them and you.

These first few years will help shape their personalities. Both parents must work together, with the same rules for your kid, as they soon learn to play you off against each other. This also keeps the arguments between you and your partner to a minimum.

As a family, I earned just enough for my wife to be a full-time mum, which was great. It gave our little family consistency and stability. In many instances, parents both work and use a multitude of different people to support, from childminders, afterschool clubs and grandparents. Again, consistency is key. It is no good making sure your little Timmy only has chocolate once a day if granny lets him fill his boots every Tuesday and Wednesday evening,

Another potential issue is that working parents can feel guilty about working. When they finally get home, they just want their kid to be happy, so they give them everything they want, buying them presents every weekend. But this is not good in the long run. It is a rather slippery slope....

The **TIPS**

1) Don't give your child everything they ask for. They will grow up to be a spoilt brat who expects everything without working for it. Birthday's, Christmas and as a reward for doing something really good or being brave, that's about it.

2) Don't be afraid to use the word no. See point number one.

3) Allowing them to run around and be free all the time, letting them do what they want all the time with no structure or ground rules, is not a good idea. Yes, I am talking to you, the lazy parents who allow their kids to run around restaurants screaming and bumping into other families who are trying to enjoy their meal. Get a grip, you idiots, stop being selfish and teach your kids some manners.

It's all about balance and consistency. If you give your kid an ultimatum about bad behaviour or the proverbial carrot ref good behaviour, please go through with it. This will provide them with the ground rules of life. Do something right, and you will get praise and possibly a treat, do something bad, and there will be consequences, e.g., the loss of a toy for a few hours or no chocolate treat after dinner. Kids need to know where the boundaries are. No boundaries, no sense of right or wrong.

Please also teach them good manners, to say please when asking for something, thank you when you give them something. No please, no treat.

The next thing is encouragement and praise.

Encourage them to work hard and praise them for doing so. Whether it is doing a piece of homework or playing football, it is all about the effort they put in, and for you to recognise this and praise accordingly.

On the flip side of this, please don't shout or get frustrated when they don't put the effort in. Try and understand why they didn't try as hard as they should have.

Did they feel unwell? Just not up for it? Too tired? Loss of interest? But it is how you react to them that is crucial.

So, here's a scenario for you

Your son/daughter has just come off the pitch after an awful game of football. They messed up a few passes, which affected their confidence, so they made more mistakes, all in all, not a great day.

How do you deal with it?

1) Tell them that was crap and that they must try harder next time
2) Ask them if anything was bothering them
3) Suggest practising passing with you so that they are more confident next time.

Please don't make choice 1) this will put them under more pressure and could actually make things worse.

Choice 2) is better. Try to understand how they felt before, during, and after the game, then work out the best way to help and encourage them. To help them to be able to deal with their feelings more confidently.

Choice 3) this will help them have more confidence, and they may even start enjoying football again.

Nobody likes to make mistakes and let the team down. It is so important that our kids learn how to deal with the negative emotions generated from this situation.

This is why they lose interest and don't want to play anymore. They lose confidence, it becomes a chore, and they simply don't enjoy it anymore. As parents, we sometimes want our kids to do a particular sport or activity because we did it or we think they should do it.

More **TIPS**

1) Let them know it's perfectly natural to mess up occasionally

2) Tell them not to dwell on the negative feeling that the mistake can cause. It's done. You can't change it. But they can learn from it.

3) Reaffirm to them that they can do it in the future.

Parenthood and Relationships – Part 2

You and the missus may have had a few kids, 2,3 or even 4.

Two kids were more than enough for me. I think my wife would maybe have liked another, but not me.

Three kids would mean some significant changes. A bigger car, a bigger house may be needed, more cash is required and more than likely some more stress.

I would rather have enough to give two a good start than scrape a living with three, but you will always find a way.

Juggling finances can be tricky at times, but if you keep your kids and yourself grounded, you will be ok. Getting into debt is a bad idea, especially if you haven't got a way to get out of it.

Debt just brings even more pressure on you as a bloke.

I am very fortunate with my wife, she rarely spends on herself, and when she does, it's usually from Primark. My only real vice is running trainers, which I regularly get through. Thankfully my wife understands how much running means to me and how happy it keeps me.

Money is one of the significant potential argument points as a couple. As we have been brought up differently, we will definitely have different views on how to spend it.

Things are so damn expensive these days, especially mobile phones. You don't want your kid to be embarrassed by the phone they have, but they need to understand what is and isn't feasible. If you are struggling to put a meal on the table, don't get a top of the range iPhone for your kid, it will only make your financial situation worse.

Compromise is the name of the game. It always is. Respect your partner's point of view. You may disagree with it but respect it.

Also, pick your battles, don't fight over every little thing. You don't have to have the final say on everything!

As time goes by, your kids will grow up and start having their own lives without you. Some mothers don't handle this very well, they have spent a good chunk of their lives taking care of their kids, and when they grow up, they can feel a little empty, with a lack of purpose. This is why both parents need to make an effort to spend quality time with each other, and it also makes sense to stay in contact with friends outside of the marriage to help keep themselves sane.

It takes an effort to make things work well. Marriage is no different. If you don't practice, you lose the skills needed to have a workable marriage. You could lose interest, become bored, which can lead to you being distracted or tempted.

You got together for a reason in the first place, don't allow your relationship to disintegrate because you don't put the time and effort in.

One thing that definitely works for me is to keep talking. You may fall out over something your other half has said but don't hold a grudge. Think it over, was your partner, right? and you don't want to admit it? If so, admit it. If you were wrong and overreacted, just say sorry and mean it.

The Essentials

These are what we need to survive, quite literally.

Water – Drink plenty of it!

We cannot live without water, our bodies are made up of more than 70% water, so we need to regularly top it up. Current recommendations for water intake stand at approx. 2.5 litres a day, which seems quite a lot, but when you break it down to 10 x 250ml glasses (about one glass an hour) throughout the day, it isn't too onerous. Most of the time, we simply forget to drink water, but it works well to get into the habit of regularly drinking water throughout the day. It also gets you out of your seat to stretch your legs at least 15 times a day, 10 trips to the tap/water cooler and 5 visits to the toilet! So, win-win!

Not drinking enough water each day can lead to:

- Loss of concentration
- Tiredness & Irritability
- Headaches
- Premature ageing
- Poor digestion

Drinking water has many benefits:

- It helps to digest your food
- It helps your concentration levels
- It helps keep your joints healthy
- It helps your body get rid of waste
- It helps prevent kidney damage
- It can help promote weight loss!
- Can help combat fatigue

- Reduces high blood pressure
- Slows the ageing process!

Do your best to cut down, then cut out, the fizzy, sugary (and the diet variants) drinks, water is so much better for you!

Sleeeeeeep

This is another rather obvious one, you need a decent night's kip for your body and mind to operate effectively. Long term poor quality and insufficient quantity sleep can seriously affect your health. A good night's sleep allows your body and mind to rest and recuperate. Our lifestyle is somewhat different from our caveman ancestry. We need around seven hours of sleep each night to help keep us sane.

Many of us can struggle to get off to sleep with too many thoughts swirling through our heads, others, like me, can fall asleep in less than two minutes. The key is to keep to a routine, go to bed around the same time, and get up at the same time.

Exercise also helps to tire you out and help you sleep. The added benefit of exercise in the evening is your body continues to burn calories at a higher rate when you sleep, bonus!

Your body reacts in several negative ways if you have a poor night's sleep for an extended period:

- Mood changes
- Weakened immunity
- Memory issues

- Weight gain
- Higher blood pressure
- Poor balance/reflexes
- Early ageing

If you feel down and depressed, poor quality sleep can make things even worse, another one of those vicious circles.

To help you settle down for the night, here are some common techniques that should help

Some **TIPS**

- Avoid caffeine or alcohol late at night
- Keep a consistent routine
- Get off the phone at least 30 mins before sleeping
- Reduce stimulation
- Get some exercise in the early evening

Food and Exercise – a love/hate relationship

Most of us love food, a piece of chocolate, a biscuit, a pizza, a Chinese takeaway. Unfortunately, most of these have the nutritional value of a piece of paper. They have plenty of calorific content but very few nutrients to help our body work effectively. But they taste so damn good!

Conversely, many of us hate exercise, even though the mere thought of it can really turn us off.

The good news is if you exercise, you will have more food freedom, i.e., you can eat a little more because you are burning calories doing exercise!

The old saying "everything in moderation" is very true. i.e., two delicious hobnobs with a coffee once a day is ok, ten coffees throughout the day with a whole packet, not so good. Sugar is an addictive little shit, the more you have, the more you want, and unfortunately the diet variants of sweeteners are even worse for you. Yes, diet coke, or diet anything is pretty bad for your body as they replace the sugar with artificial sweeteners, replace the fat with God knows what, which the body struggles to digest, so, guess what, it is stored in your body, as fat.

Whilst having virtually zero calories, diet fizzy drinks aren't really a good idea because it has the same sweet taste as the sugar variant. Your brain thinks it is getting sugar with lots of calories, which it doesn't get, so it's now hungry and wants food! Yes, the diet drink potentially makes you want to eat more!

To get the best out of our bodies from a nutritional perspective, we need nutrients and vitamins from fruit and veg, carbohydrates from Pasta, rice or potatoes (to name just a few), protein from fish or meat or lentils and a small amount of fat. Yes, your body needs a proportion of fat, ideally the non-saturated variety:

Fat is an essential source of fatty acids, which the body cannot make itself. The job of fatty acid is to metabolise and absorb vitamins: A, D and E, which are fat-soluble, i.e., only fat can absorb them into your body. Good fats can also help positive brain function. But too much fat in your diet that is not used by the body's cells or turned into energy is converted into body fat, as is unused carbohydrates or protein.

Simply put:

Too much food + no exercise = weight gain + health issues.

Are you happy with your body shape? Are you carrying a "few" extra pounds? Do you look in the mirror and say, yup, looking good? If not, you probably need to reconsider your food and exercise routine. I.e., do some exercise, stop eating everything in the house, or conversely cut down on excessive exercise and eat healthily.

If you are out of breath after walking up the stairs, you either have terrible asthma, or you really need to start to exercise and eat less!

I will rephrase this, if you are overweight, feel lethargic, and have low self-esteem, this is surely enough to get you moving?

You probably know you should do some exercise, but you are probably far too comfortable, or is the thought of exercise more uncomfortable than the sight you see in the mirror?

Yes, exercise can be hard work, but the benefits are pretty long-reaching, not only physically but mentally, it is sooooo good for you:

Physical Benefits

- **An improved immune system**
- **Better weight control**
- More muscle strength and muscle mass (which helps burn calories and fat)
- **Increased energy levels**
- Improved flexibility and movement
- Strength training & weight-bearing exercise promotes stronger bones
- Increased "good" cholesterol to keep blood flowing smoothly
- **Lower risk of a heart attack and stroke**
- Can help smokers quit with higher success rates
- It can reduce your risk of major illnesses, such as heart disease, stroke, type 2 diabetes and cancer by up to 50% and lower your risk of early death by up to 30%

Mental health Benefits

- Up to a 30% lower risk of depression
- Up to a 30% lower risk of dementia
- **Regular exercise has been shown equal to antidepressant use in treating Major Depressive Disorder**
- Regular aerobic exercise increases levels of serotonin and dopamine in the brain, which is linked with improved mood
- Aerobic exercise increases endorphins, or the "feel good" chemicals in the body, improving mood and energy
- **Enhances the mind's ability to withstand daily hassles and stressors and to regulate itself**
- Exercise is associated with deeper relaxation and better quality of sleep (which protects the brain and increases energy)
- Strength training has been shown to decrease tension and worry in the body and mind
- **Studies show exercise reduces and may help prevent anxiety and panic attacks**
- Exercise increases mental clarity and efficiency
- Improves cognitive functioning in middle age and beyond
- Exercise is associated with better thinking, learning, and judgment
- It can help you tap into intuition and creativity
- Exercise increases assertiveness and enthusiasm for life
- Studies show exercise leads to a higher-quality sex life

- **Group or partner exercise increases social activity and decreases feelings of loneliness and isolation**
- Those who exercise regularly tend to have a better body image
- Regular exercise is associated with higher self-esteem
- **Overall,** *exercise is one of the best ways to improve happiness and life satisfaction*

So enough of the usual excuses: I don't have the time, I'm too tired (because you don't exercise, you muppet), just get out there and do it!

You don't have to run a marathon; start by walking briskly three times a week for at least 30 minutes, then try running and walking. Check out the couch to 5km programs online, then just get on with it and follow them!

Another important reason to keep exercising is that our metabolic rate decreases as we age, which is the rate at which our body uses energy.

As kids, we have a high metabolic rate as our bodies need a lot of energy to develop and grow. From the age of twenty onwards, we have reached physical maturity and our metabolic rate decreases by 1-2% a decade. By the time we reach our fifties, the rate of decline increases at an even higher rate. This is also to do with the number of new cells our bodies are producing. Because as we age, the renewing process slows, which means the body needs less energy to produce fewer cells.

Muscle mass is also a factor. After you hit thirty, this can decline between 3-5% a decade. With less muscle mass, your body needs less energy. So, this basically means if you keep eating the same amount, you will put weight on, as your body doesn't have the muscle mass it once had (which needed a decent amount of energy). So, start doing the press-ups and squats now! Keep that muscle mass!

If you keep eating at the same rate and quantity in our 30/40/50/60's as you did when you were in your twenties, and you don't do any exercise, you are basically going to gain a couple of pounds here and there every year. Before you know it, you are struggling to fit into an airplane seat, and you only wear jogger bottoms and sweatshirts.

From a food intake point of view, it's all about your calorific intake. For us blokes, our bodies need 2500 calories each day (on average) to function. If we sit all day on our arse and don't do more than 100 steps, we probably won't need this much.

If you consume more than 2500 calories and do no exercise, you will definitely gain weight. It's that simple.

If you consume less than 2500 calories and do no exercise, you will lose weight, but if you exercise, the rate at which you lose weight will be greater.

If you exercise, your body will need more energy, use more calories to retain or even gain muscle mass. If you maintain an intake of 2500, you will lose weight because you are using more than 2500 each day.

The more vigorous or out of breath you are during a sporting activity, the more calories you burn.

It's useful to keep a record of your daily calorie intake (MyFitnessPal is an excellent app to track calories) as there are a surprising number of calories in many of our everyday foods, especially those sweet snacks, and they all mount up. A decent sized pizza is 1000 calories, a chocolate bar is around 150, a slice of bread, a singular slice of bread is about 90 calories. Don't even get me started on alcohol, specifically beer or lager, at around 150-250 calories a pint. It soon mounts up on a Friday and Saturday night, week after week.

To help keep the weight gain in check, exercise, and ensure food restraint, i.e., stay within your daily recommended intake of calories.

If you go over this and don't exercise, you will gain weight. If you go under the limit and do no exercise, you will lose weight (slowly, which is good), but you can have a net loss of weight by exercising a certain amount to get a win-win situation.

You can even go a little over your intake figure as long as there is a NET loss.

E.g., For a bloke weighing 80kg, to burn/use 500 calories, you would need to either:

- Swim for an hour, or,
- Cycle for 50mins, or
- Weight train for 1hr 45 mins, or
- Walk for 1hr 45 mins, or
- Run for 32 mins at a quick pace (7.5mph)

Running is one of the highest calorific burning exercises.

If you consume 2700 calories in a day, then run for 32 mins at 7.5 mph (-500), your net intake is 2200 calories or what they call a "net Deficit", leading to weight loss, simples.

I will be blunt, get off your arse, and do some exercise. You will feel better, look better and move better, fact.

You can also reduce your risk of developing heart and circulatory disease by as much as 35% by being more active.

Choice time

The **HITS**

Make a positive change, get some exercise, stop the takeaways and the beer for a while, look after yourself. Feel better about yourself, start enjoying life again

Or

The **SHITS**

Continue as you are, eat more, drink more, have a nice heart attack, become a burden to your family, feel like shit, look like shit.

The **TIPS**

One of the best ways to start exercising is to find an exercise buddy, someone who has a similar goal, to whom you commit to meeting up with for whatever exercise you want to do. Whether it's walking, running, swimming or cycling. If you can commit to at least 3 x 30 min exercise sessions a week, you will see and feel the positive benefits within three months, and if you make it to three months, you will have created a healthy habit.

Companionship & Friendship

We all crave attention. We want to be listened to, acknowledged, noticed, even admired. A lot of this may be down to the fact that we are all slightly insecure and need others' attention to help prove to ourselves that we are not entirely useless.

There are many different types of friends; those you don't see much, those you see a little of, those you see all the time, those you can depend on to be there for you when you need them most.

We naturally gravitate to people with similar values and interests and move away from those we clash with. True friends will always be there for you, to talk to when things are tough, and be there to share the good times as well.

A true friend accepts you for who you are, who respects your opinions, even if they disagree with them. A friend will want to know how you are feeling, how you are doing, and are genuinely interested in your well-being.

To fully engage with others, we just need to be ourselves, our true, unabashed, raw, stupid selves. Many people out there are more bothered about how they are perceived by others, how they look, and how "popular" they are. If you put on an outwardly "perfect" persona but are actually deeply unhappy and dissatisfied with life, it means you need to drop the false image and just be the real you. It's a lot less tiring and stressful.

It's good to talk

Now you may be thinking that this chapter doesn't belong in a section titled the "essentials", but I would like to ask you to reconsider.

Without the opportunity to talk over our day, our highs & lows, we only have our own voices in our head for company. If these voices are negative, this can dramatically affect our sense of well-being, confidence, mood, and behaviour.

Talking is even more critical when we are struggling. It really is ok to ask for help. You are not failing, there is nothing to be ashamed about, you are just having a bit of a shit time, and talking it through with someone can really help.

The longer you go without talking, the harder it is to speak up, it just intensifies the feelings of helplessness, and you start to withdraw from all aspects of life. Because in your head, you believe that no one will want to know or care. So, the best thing to do is get it off your chest as early as possible, then you can nip it in the bud before it gets worse.

The happy flow is that most people love to help. A true friend will actually be honoured that you have approached them. It's all about trust.

Just call up someone you can trust and ask, "have you got time to chat for 15 mins? I just really need to talk about something that is bothering me". Nine times out of ten, they will say yes, sure. But if they are a little busy, ask them when would be a good time for them? If they then say, really sorry, got shit loads on, that's ok. Don't take it personally, they may be distracted or having a tough time themselves, just call friend number 2.

If we keep everything to ourselves, it starts to fester and get worse, you start worrying about it even more, and without an outlet to get it off your chest, it can become rather debilitating.

I know you may think that your friend might have their own worries, but sharing yours will allow them to share theirs too, so it's a win-win situation. Chances are your friend will have been in a similar situation before, and they can relate to your predicament and give you some pertinent advice.

Smiling and Laughter

A certain Elf said, "Smiling's my favourite".

There have been many scientific studies concerning the benefits of smiling. Smiling not only improves your own mood but can also positively affect the mood of those around you.

There is also a strong link between good health and longevity with smiling.

Here are several excellent reasons why you should keep smiling

- it makes you feel good.
- It helps you stay positive.
- It makes you look younger.
- It relieves stress.
- It elevates your mood.
- It is contagious.
- It boosts your immune system.
- It lowers your blood pressure.

So don't be that miserable twat that never smiles. If you act miserable, you will remain miserable, your outlook will remain negative.

Now, laughter, cliché time again, "laughter is the best medicine".

Being able to share laughter is priceless. To be able to laugh at yourself is also healthy.

We often take ourselves far too seriously or judge ourselves too harshly. We so readily get offended by other people's opinions or statements. Getting ourselves into arguments for no real reason whatsoever, usually over the most stupid little things.

So, please don't take yourself too seriously. A daft or insensitive comment is simply that, just let it wash over you, just smile and move on, much better.

Laughter can lift your mood and that of others immensely, whether at a daft joke or just something someone has said that most people wouldn't have laughed at, but it had you in a fit of the giggles.

My most vivid memory of a massive laughing fit was whilst at uni. I was in a lecture on Electrical theory, not the most exciting of subjects, which was made worse because the lecturer, whilst a nice bloke, had the most monotone voice ever (picture the teacher in Ferris Buellers day off, Bueller, Bueller). Approximately halfway through the lecture, there was a change of subject, the title of which was Electrical Power trains, to which my mate Chris, who was sitting beside me, did a little high-pitched Choo Choo under his breath.

And that was me gone, I was off, I simply could not stop laughing, and by trying to suppress the giggles, my stomach was actually hurting. I was literally crying with laughter, I just couldn't stop, then just as I got myself under control, I would look at Chris, and I was off again, best lecture ever.

It's ok to be daft occasionally, to be able to raise a smile is a wonderful thing. Life is too short to be serious all the time.

Life's constants

These are the things that are always there, marching on. You can't avoid them or stop them, just hang on and make the best of them.

Time

So many cliches, so little time. The most common one is spot on: "there is no time like the present", another rather pertinent one: "time waits for no man".

The present is in our hands, the past is gone, the future is out there, waiting for us.

We can't stop time, rewind or fast forward it. We just need to appreciate and be thankful that we have another day. Another day to make a positive difference in our lives and others. We have a finite amount of time to do all the stuff we want to do. How we spend our time is one of the most important things we have to think about.

We usually whinge that we haven't got enough time, but the truth is, the only reason we haven't got enough time is that we fill our day with pointless shit.

We spend the day moaning about others, we spend it saying we haven't got enough time, we spend too many hours on our phones reading mindless crap, watching mindless videos, playing mindless games.

We treat our phones as a welcome distraction to the world we live in. We use them to ignore the realities of the world and our responsibilities. We crave short term wins for the least amount of effort possible. We think only of ourselves, not how our actions could affect others.

We have become selfish arseholes.

We crave our social media, yet we don't really engage with the people around us.

Social media is a bit of a bad joke. It should be called antisocial media. It's full of wannabees, and moaners, and liars. It's a mindless stream of "entertainment". There is no end to the distraction, there is always another video clip to watch.

We struggle to see the real world. We don't want to see it most of the time.

What I am trying to say is to use your time more productively. When it's gone, it's gone.

Let's say the average person lives to be 80 years old, you probably don't know much about the first 4 years, and you won't be able to do much in your last couple of years, so that's you down to 73.

- You spend a $1/3^{rd}$ of your life sleeping (if you're lucky),
- Another $1/3$ at work (If you're lucky/unlucky depending on your perspective),
- So that leaves $1/3$ to do stuff you want to do, roughly 24 years.

So that leaves 7 hours a day, sounds a lot, but if you spend a couple of hours on your mobile, an hour eating that's you down to 4hrs, not a great deal of time.

- How much of your time do you spend doing pointless shit?
- How much much of your time do you give to others? Too little or too much?

- How much quality time do you spend with your kids or your significant other?

I realise now that I have spent far too much time playing games on my mobile, I must have spent days on sodding candy crush, I can't get those hours back. The only way I have stopped wasting my time on them is to delete them.

To help myself actually get something done each day, I use a reminder planner to allocate time to different tasks throughout the day, then incentivise myself to complete them. It's good to be realistic and factor in some nothing time to relax and chill out.

One of the greatest gifts you can give to another is your time. To be there for a friend who is struggling and wants to talk. This is an hour well spent, I would say it is priceless.

It can mean so much to someone when you are there to give them time to talk and have someone to listen to them.

Another time sucker is our tendency to dwell on the shit from the past. You can't change what has happened, so don't relive it daily, beating yourself up about a past transgression or event will only serve to make you upset, bitter and more unhappy.

Please don't let a previous lousy situation stop you from living for today and the future.

You can't have a better tomorrow if you are thinking about yesterday all the time. (Charles F. Kettering, an American inventor, engineer, businessman, and the holder of 186 patents*)*

Our time is a finite resource, and the real kick in the bollocks is that we don't know exactly how much time we have to play with. We could have thirty years left, or two years, or two months. We never know what is around the corner, so isn't it best to make every minute count?

We only exist in the present, not the past or the future. Whatever you choose to do now will affect your future. So, try and make it a good choice. Continually bad or unhealthy choices rarely result in a rosy future. Stop and think about what you are about to say or do, even just for a second, will it make things better or worse? Again, your choice.

Many people are suffering from chronic illnesses or cancer, who may have a much-shortened lifespan, so please try and be grateful for each day and having the ability to enjoy it. Many others are not so fortunate.

Will you look back on your life and say, yes, I made good use of my time, made a positive difference, or shit, I spent far too much time pissing about liking pointless shit on Facebook.

So, isn't it time you looked up from your mobile, and appreciated what is around you and make the most of it, rather than ignoring it or missing the moment completely?

I see so many people walking around with their attention firmly on their phones, not even looking where they are going, never mind appreciating what is happening around them.

Choice time:

The **HITS**

Make good use of your time. Make time to help other people less fortunate than yourself.

or

The **SHITS**

Do your own thing all the time, waste your time away on pointless shit, spend all of your time looking at your mobile, end up regretting that you did nothing worthwhile in your life.

Change

Such an innocuous word, change. Change lanes, change our pants, change the way we feel about people and change our jobs.

Change is a part of life.

Change is inevitable, persistent and ever-present.

Every day is different, we react in different ways, we change our way of thinking depending upon the events of the day, for better or worse.

Sometimes change is forced upon us, other times, it happens naturally.

We usually only change for the better when something becomes too unbearable not to change. However, it can take quite a long time to get this hint as we are generally well stuck in our ways.

Change can also be scary when you are comfortable in what you do and where you are in life. It's not too difficult to keep the status quo if you are ok with doing the same thing day in day out.

But you could accomplish so much more if you got out of your comfort zone and tried something new, tried to do something that you never thought would be possible. But if you don't try, you will never know what you can be capable of.

Sometimes it takes a life-changing event for you to change, like a heart attack at the age of 49, probably caused by the 20 cigs a day, the 20 pints of lager every weekend and the fact that you are 10 stone overweight.

But if you really opened your eyes to see how bad things were getting and actually did something about it before it gets to the heart attack stage, then this would be soooo much better for you and your family.

Again, this is related to having confidence in yourself, your self-image and your comfort zone. If you don't have the confidence to try new things, you will continue doing the same thing, day in, day out.

If you have a low opinion of yourself and don't want to push yourself for fear of failure, you won't know what it's like to feel the joy of achieving something new.

I am pretty sure the key to trying out new things and pushing yourself out of your comfort zone comes down to one thing.

Worrying about what other people might think, what they could say to put you off if they see you trying out something new, or chasing a new dream.

This is called a limiting belief. It's limiting you from doing something out of the belief that their opinion matters.

It only matters what you think, not what they think. If you want to do it, do it. Or you may well spend the rest of your life regretting that you didn't even try.

The real kick in the bollocks is that you become angry with yourself and others for the way this has "made you feel", but it's because you let it, not anyone else.

I know it's tough to try new things and try something different, but it's worth pushing through the initial fear and doubt. Because if you try it out and it doesn't work out, you know that it wasn't for you. If you don't try, you will never know.

For example:

You love fruit scones with butter on them, and you think it's the only way to eat fruit scones. Someone suggests adding Strawberry jam, you like jam but not on scones. So, you don't try it.

Eventually, you try it, and it's even better than with just butter on. You kick yourself for not trying it earlier; this is a metaphor for change; by embracing and trying out a new idea, you can change your perception and awareness.

We are all hit with the doubts of change daily, if not hourly. But it is so worth it when you dare to give it a go. It is really rather scary at first, but then you start to enjoy the tingle of excitement that it brings, and the fear starts to change to enjoyment.

If you are bored with life, try changing a small part of it, then a bit more, then a bit more! You will be amazed at what you can achieve with some optimism and faith in your abilities.

Choice time:

The **HITS**

Chase your dreams, try out new things, find fulfilment in new and exciting places

or

The **SHITS**

Never try anything new.

Become more miserable, bitter, twisted.

Blame it all on everyone else, take no ownership whatsoever for your current situation, get more and more pissed off.

Ageing and our own Mortality

We are only on this earth for a relatively short time. It's how we use
this time that is the crucial bit. We are not gods. We do not live
forever. Having life also means at some point, we won't.

They say life is wasted on the young, but this is only said by
older blokes who have regrets that they didn't do enough when
they were younger.

As shown below, there are many causes of death, the biggest
being cardiovascular disease. Of the 17.79 million deaths
worldwide in 2019, 92% was in the over 50 age group.

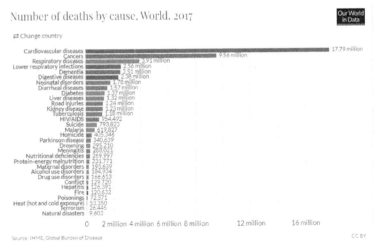

Number of deaths by cause, World, 2017

The most significant risk of death is from the following factors:

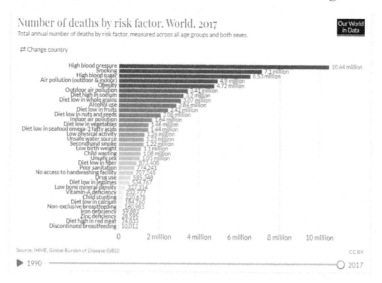

Number of deaths by risk factor, World, 2017
Total annual number of deaths by risk factor, measured across all age groups and both sexes.

Our World in Data

⇄ Change country

High blood pressure — 10.44 million
Smoking — 7.1 million
High blood sugar — 6.53 million
Air pollution (outdoor & indoor) — 4.9 million
Obesity — 4.72 million
Outdoor air pollution — 3.41 million
Diet high in sodium — 3.2 million
Diet low in whole grains — 3.07 million
Alcohol use — 2.84 million
Diet low in fruits — 2.42 million
Diet low in nuts and seeds — 2.06 million
Indoor air pollution — 1.64 million
Diet low in vegetables — 1.46 million
Diet low in seafood omega-3 fatty acids — 1.44 million
Low physical activity — 1.26 million
Unsafe water source — 1.23 million
Secondhand smoke — 1.22 million
Low birth weight — 1.1 million
Child wasting — 1.08 million
Unsafe sex — 1.03 million
Diet low in fiber — 873,406
Poor sanitation — 774,241
No access to handwashing facility — 707,248
Drug use — 585,348
Diet low in legumes — 534,767
Low bone mineral density — 327,314
Vitamin-A deficiency — 232,777
Child stunting — 220,679
Diet low in calcium — 184,760
Non-exclusive breastfeeding — 150,983
Iron deficiency — 59,867
Zinc deficiency — 28,595
Diet high in red meat — 24,835
Discontinued breastfeeding — 10,012

0   2 million   4 million   6 million   8 million   10 million

Source: IHME, Global Burden of Disease (GBD)

CC BY

▶ 1990 ——————————————————————○ 2017

As you can see, unless you have hereditary high blood pressure, the top 3 causes of death can be reduced with a decent diet and exercise.

At number five, Obesity kills nearly 5 million people every year. Again, this can be massively reduced with a decent diet and regular exercise.

When we are in our teens, we don't even think about our own mortality. It is not even on our radar.

As we move from our twenties into our thirties, we still think we are pretty young and invincible. We don't really care what we eat or drink, inhale or inject. But all the time we shovel shit into our bodies, it is doing long-term damage, then suddenly, we turn forty. This one stings a bit. This doesn't sound young. You are now officially a grown-up or should be. Many blokes hit forty, look in the mirror and think, whoa, how the hell did I turn into this eighteen stone fat lad? I was only twelve stone last year, well, maybe a few years ago.

This is usually when we begin to start looking after ourselves a little more, maybe sort our diet out and even take up some form of exercise. The later in life we leave this, the harder it is to turn the tide to some sort of healthiness.

If you hit fifty and you are up to twenty stone, FFS, do something now. You can still do something about it unless you are too lazy or have zero respect for yourself.

In our fifties, we become aware that people we know and love start to pass away, an old boss, an uncle, even a parent, which should be even more of a wake-up call. Also, not everyone we went to school with is still walking this planet.

This is when we start realising, we are not going to live forever. This is when we need to get our shit together and make the most of our time left, as we don't know what is around the corner.

By the time we hit sixty, our bodies are starting to slow us down. We have more aches and pains and start groaning when we get up. We start thinking about retirement more and more, firming up plans to have a comfortable next 20 years (hopefully). But for some of us, it's too late. We have spent all our lives working hard, playing hard, providing for our families, dealing with our day-to-day stresses then, have a heart attack or a stroke, and die.

This happened to one of my old bosses. His lifelong habit of smoking probably played a large part in this. He retired in his early 60s and, within a year, had passed away.

This is really rather sad. Imagine working till you are sixty-five, then kick the bucket when you should be relaxing and enjoying yourself. With us having kids later on in life these days than our parents and grandparents, we could miss seeing our kids live their adult lives and miss those special moments with our grandkids. Why would your self-sabotage yourself so much that these were the consequences?

This is why we need to make the most of our time whilst we are fit and able to do so, don't leave it till it's too late #repeatingmyself

So when are you going to wake up? When will you do something about your diet, your lack of exercise, your smoking habit? Tomorrow is too bloody late.

If you keep abusing your body, you could die early, leaving your wife and kids to struggle on without you. All because you couldn't be bothered to get up off your arse and prioritised beer, takeaways and maybe cigarettes above a healthy diet and exercise.

I know it's challenging to change the habits of a lifetime but imagine one of your good friends died of a heart attack, leaving his wife and kids fending for themselves, trying to make ends meet, do you really want to put your own family through that?

Choice time:

The HITS

Make positive changes to your lifestyle so that you have the opportunity to live a long and happy life

Or

The SHITS

Keep abusing your body, feel tired and pissed off all the time, age quicker, die younger.

The **TIPS**

Start with small changes

Month 1 -   Cut out alcohol Sunday to Thursday

Month 2 -   Continue the above and cut down on the
             takeaways to once or twice per month

Month 3 -   Continue the above and cut down on the sweet
             treats like cake and chocolate

Month 4 -   Continue the above and get some exercise &
             keep exercising

Month 5 →   Do all of the above every month from now on.

The Shits

Daily challenges to be accepted and overcome

Each day there will be some sort of challenge, a task at work, a deadline to be met, bad news may arrive about an ill friend, or you get the news that your company has to fold.

This is entirely normal and part of life, but it is how we deal with it that matters.

Negative Opinion

We have to deal with this daily, whether from the boss, the missus or our "friends". And now there's all the negativity on social media.

We can usually deal with the odd bit of negativity, but it can really affect us when it becomes a never-ending daily occurrence. This is why it is important to have a circle of friends with a positive, supportive disposition rather than those with a constant negative outlook.

The more you get negative comments the more you start to believe them, which makes you question what you are doing and how you do it. You then find yourself altering how you do things so that you don't get negative comments.

This has a massive effect on our self-confidence, especially when trying new ways of doing something. If you get laughed at or mocked for trying something new, it really puts you off from trying again.

The only real way to deal with a negative opinion is to ignore it. It is only an opinion. It is not the truth. It is just somebody else's viewpoint, which they give through their own eyes and experiences. Basically, if they see you doing something different to what they would do, they can feel the need to reinforce their own beliefs, which could mean belittling yours, which is really rather shit.

Everyone would get along a hell of a lot better with each other (and have a lot fewer arguments) if they just accepted that other people have different experiences, viewpoints and thoughts. That they aren't trying to prove you wrong, it's just their opinion!

So, my advice is not to let your ego drive your mouth. Don't feel the need to "prove" you are right or criticise someone for doing something you would never do.

The benefit of accepting other people's viewpoints (and I am not saying you have to agree with them) is that you will reduce your own stress levels. You won't bite back and hopefully not get into a usually pointless argument over bugger all.

Frustration

We all get frustrated on a daily basis, probably on an hourly basis. We get frustrated with the weather, the boss, our own abilities (or lack of), the fact that we had a holiday cancelled, so many opportunities for us to get pissed off.

When we get frustrated, we stop thinking clearly and usually overreact. We get upset, angry, and typically lash out verbally at anyone in the immediate vicinity.

We usually blame other people when our frustration bubbles over, but our inability to deal with the situation is the root of the problem.

2020 was the mother of all frustration, thanks to a little virus called covid19. We had lockdowns, holiday cancellations, job losses, the loss of loved ones, the loss of our freedom, the inability to do what we wanted when we wanted.

But most of this is out of our control, which really stung, we usually only do our best to deal with the things we can control the situation. But when we are not in control, it does our head in.

So how do we help ourselves not become so annoyed?

We simply need to accept that not everything will go our way, or the way we think it should go. Shit happens. Once it has happened, you can't change it, so why do we get so pissed off? Primarily because of our ego or our feelings.

So when you feel your blood starting to boil, just stop, take 10 big deep breaths, pause, take another 10. Now, this should have calmed you down a little bit and allowed your brain to catch up, think about whether it's really worth making a massive fuss about.

I am sure the thing you were about to get upset about is either out of your control or relatively inconsequential in the grand scheme of things.

For example, one of my passions is running. I get very frustrated when I am injured and need to stop running and rest for a week or so (if I am lucky). Running is a massive part of my life. It helps me feel good about myself, it clears my mind and gives me some sense of freedom.

When I am injured, I get impatient and really rather cranky with the time needed for the healing process to do its job so that I can run again. But being pissed off doesn't do anything other than stress me out. By accepting that these things happen and that I need to be patient and let my body heal, then I can stop feeling quite so annoyed.

I have to remind myself that I am lucky that I can still move around and do my day-to-day tasks. Many people have severe, debilitating conditions. This gives me some perspective, and I calm down and get on with it.

Let's stop being a bit of a drama queen and calm the hell down. Stop the drama, stop the indignation, stop your ego from driving your thoughts and your mouth.

Just stay calm, and carry on.

This takes practice, lots of practice, but it is very worthwhile, as once you get the hang of not overreacting to absolutely everything, life is a lot less frantic and stressful.

Temptation – the grass isn't always greener

There are many forms of temptation out there, ready to pounce. It sometimes takes real, firm willpower to resist.

Whether that temptation is to have another biscuit, another beer, another glass of wine. It is so easy to give in for that blissful quick hit of instant gratification. It's only when we notice we can't fit into our jeans anymore that we realise we shouldn't really readily give into temptation.

I believe we give in to temptation to feel good for just a few short moments. The issue is when we rely on these fleeting moments. Then everything else becomes a tedious unbearable situation.

Temptation usually strikes when we are feeling down, dissatisfied and pissed off. Whether it is concerning our jobs, our relationships or our diets. We start looking for ways to stop feeling bad about ourselves and our situation. The problem is if we try the temporary fix, i.e., a new job or a new partner, it isn't really solving the issue you were dissatisfied with in the first place, i.e., you.

Life is difficult. It is very rarely "easy". If it was easy all the time, we would more than likely become bored and dissatisfied, and then temptation would jump up in front of us, waving its big red flag. Then off you go again, looking for another panacea, another perfect job, partner, diet.

This endless search to find happiness invariably leads to disappointment because happiness is not a destination. It is not a target to be achieved. Why? Because it's almost impossible to achieve a sustained status of happiness.

You hear it all the time. If I had a new job, I would be so much happier. If I could afford to go to New York this Christmas, that would make me happy.

But the truth is we would be temporarily happy or feel less shit, but if you don't change your outlook on life, you would once again soon be back where you started, the "I need a new job situation", Groundhog Day.

So how do we stop ourselves from being tempted by one more biscuit, the cute lass in the pub, the beer in the fridge?

We need to take a real good, honest look at ourselves and understand why we feel dissatisfied. If you are unhappy in your job or relationship, look at how you can improve things rather than just jumping ship.

We should look at the bigger picture, we need to confirm our long-term goals, and if the short-term gratification helps us towards those goals, then that's ok. If they don't, well, don't do it.

To help us achieve our goals, we need a well-defined reason for doing them. Does the pain of not reaching our long-term goal outweigh the short-term gratification?

To do this, we need to break our bad habits and create productive new ones. Only then can we become more at ease with ourselves and more satisfied in general.

Procrastination

Procrastination is a natural human trait and so natural and effortless that we do it all the time.

Tomorrow is procrastination's best mate. I'll do it tomorrow, tomorrow I will start my diet. I'll call Mark and sort it out tomorrow. These are the things we always say, and very little gets done.

We know we should get off our arse and do it, but we will find a multitude of reasons not to do it. In fact, we will find other things to do just so we can put off what we need to do!

We are also very susceptible to distraction. It's another mechanism of procrastination.

One of the biggest distractions is our mobile phone, the almost endless notifications from so many different apps. When our friend posts on FB or Instagram, a "like" to one of our posts. We have become rather needy beings, becoming reliant on "likes". We even feel dejected when we don't get "likes" and only become happy when we get some.

If it is the difference between getting something done that we really don't want to do, like repainting all the internal doors, or getting an instant hit of gratification from a post "like", the post wins every time.

So how do we become better at getting things done?

We need to minimize distractions. My eldest daughter leaves her mobile phone downstairs whilst she revises upstairs, which really helped her focus.

Another way to stop procrastination and actually get things done is...

Accountability

If we commit to someone else what we plan to do, and when we will do it, we are much more likely to commit to carrying it out and have a far higher chance of actually getting it done.

Writing down the tasks, saying them aloud, and keeping them in sight wherever you spend the most time can really help. Another trick is to break the task down into smaller chunks, bitesize pieces if you like.

Also, be realistic with your to-do list of tasks and their timeframes. Otherwise, you will get dejected when you don't complete them and never get them done.

For example, if you say I am going to get a new job in the next three months, you need to break this down into a number of parts, let's call these core tasks:

- Update your CV
- Write down a list of things you don't like about your current position
- Write down what things you do like about your current role
- Write down the things that you are good at.
- Write down the kind of things you would like to do in the future.
- Start applying for applicable jobs

This all helps focus your mind, and once you have completed each task, this should give you a sense of well-being and encourage you to do the rest of the tasks because you like this feeling.

Fear and Doubt

Fear and doubt are the biggest killers of ideas, hopes and aspirations. The fear of the unknown, fear of not being good enough, fear of fucking it up.

We all too readily base our current decisions on past failures rather than with optimism of what could be the possible future. It all comes back to self-confidence and self-esteem. If you have a low level of both, you will probably have many doubts and a negative outlook. The flip side is that if you push through the fear, face it, ignore the inner doubts, and just get on with it, believe you can do it. This gives you self-confidence!

As a teenager, I was almost in a constant state of fear and doubt. I was fearful of what the school bullies would have in store for me each school day, doubting my ability to get my school work done to a decent standard. I had very little self-confidence as a result, thankfully my parents put me into a judo class, and I got some confidence back. Another confidence boost was that I went to another school to join their orchestra (ours didn't have one), and I made some great friends and actually got out of my shell and enjoyed myself.

It's essential to get some small wins under our belts, build on these wins, show ourselves that we can succeed and actually do it. We need to hold on to these successes and use them to have the confidence to continue to keep giving it a go, to throw caution to the wind and embrace the possibilities of what could be.

It's also imperative to accept that it may not work out the first time you try. In fact, you have at least a 50/50 chance you will fail.

But please don't be put off trying again. By persisting, practicing, trying a different way of getting to your goal, all of this will make you stronger and more resilient. When you finally achieve your goal, you will understand what can be achieved, which will give you the confidence to take on many more challenges.

So, go on, take a chance, follow your gut feeling, just do it. It's so worth it when you can get rid of those shackles of doubt and genuinely enjoy the experiences that it can bring.

To summarise

- Getting out of your comfort zone is a good thing
- Believe in yourself, not others' opinions of you.
- To enable change, a want for the change is needed

Choice Time

The **HITS**

Believe that you can do it, push yourself, ignore the naysayers

or

The **SHITS**

Remain scared and afraid, allow doubt to limit your potential

The **Tips**

- Start with trying something new once a week, then twice a week. This gets you out of your comfort zone and gives you more confidence
- Commit to a task/project with a set timeframe and share with a trusted friend to make you accountable
- JFDI (Just fucking do it).

Regret

Regret is such a pointless waste of time.

Life can be short and unpredictable, so don't leave it too late to say sorry to someone that you have fallen out with in the past.

Someone you may have really got on with but fell out over something stupid. Would it not be better to get in contact with them and see how they are doing? I am sure they would appreciate you contacting them. If something happened to them and you didn't get a chance to speak with them again, would that be upsetting? If so, just call them!

A lot of the time, our ego gets in the way of us being honest with ourselves. We don't like our version of the truth to be questioned, and we take it personally when someone says something contrary to our beliefs.

If someone calls you out on something you have done and it's true, don't act offended, upset, or angry. Just hold your hand up and say yes, and if appropriate, say sorry.

Another type of regret is when you haven't done something that you always wanted to, for example, wishing you had learnt the piano, wishing you had walked up Ben Nevis, regretting that you never did get to Switzerland.

We will find many excuses not to something because it's usually easier to do nothing and a lot easier to just whine about it. It takes effort and planning to do something you really want to do, and this puts us off because most of us just want an easy life.

Do you really want to get to your 80s and be the old man in the nursing home who is always saying, I wish I... or I regret not......

Make a plan to do what you have always wanted to do, save the money needed, allocate the necessary time to achieve it. If you don't plan and never actually start doing something towards it, you will most likely never do it.

Once again, you have one life. Start living it FFS!

Stop finding excuses, stop finding other things to do, which means you have even more reasons not to get on with it. Start working towards your dreams, your passions. A natural by-product of working towards a goal is that you will find you start enjoying life more because you actually have a purpose, something to aim for. Don't be put off by the obstacles that might get in your way. Life is like that, just adjust your plan accordingly and keep moving forward, don't stop, because if you do, you will probably never achieve your dreams.

When your hopes are dashed, or you give up on your dreams, it has a negative effect on your mental health and well-being. You will get frustrated, angry and miserable, and you will take it out on those around you. So not only are you Mr Sad Sack, you make those around you miserable too. Well done, not.

Choice Time

The **HITS**

Make that plan, action it, call that mate, JFDI, you will see the
benefits and actually feel good about yourself

or

The **SHITS**

Whinge about how you haven't got the time, make even more
excuses, do the same shit you have always done, be miserable.

Loneliness

Most people think of loneliness in terms of being alone, by yourself, with no significant other.

But you can also feel alone in a relationship. You may not feel that you don't connect with your partner anymore, or you don't have any close friends that you can relate to.

The dichotomy of life is that we usually want to find someone to share our life with when we are single. Then, after a few years of being with someone, you find yourself wanting to have some time alone!

As with everything in life, it's about balance.

Too much of one thing is usually bad for you in the long run. Whether that one thing is chocolate, running, coffee, work, alcohol, the list is infinite.

Once in a relationship, it's healthy that you have some differing interests, but also massively important to have some similar interests too. Otherwise, it's pretty pointless living together.

It is also crucial that you give each other some space regularly, especially if you have been arguing, but try not to go off and do something silly. That will probably just make things a whole lot worse. It has also been shown that loneliness is bad for your health:

Prolonged loneliness can lead to, or add to:

- Depressive symptoms,
- Long term effects on your self-confidence,
- hinder sleep

- weakened immunity.

It can also mean that you have a higher risk of heart disease, type 2 diabetes. It can even mean you are twice as likely to develop Alzheimer's.

It's really worth the effort to keep in touch with our friends and keep up the social interaction. I know we can sometimes lose touch with our old mates, and relationships break up, but we need that sense of belonging, whether in a group, as a couple, or with your mates. It helps us deal with life. Life can be tough enough. It is so much more challenging when you have no one to turn to.

The **Tips**

- Make a point of talking with friends and colleagues

- consider joining a group or class that focuses on something you enjoy; you could ask to go along and just watch first if you're feeling nervous
- consider visiting places where you can just be around other people – for example, a park, the cinema or a cafe
- consider peer support, where people use their experiences to help each other. Find out more about peer support on the Mind website
- find out how to raise your self-esteem
- listen to free mental wellbeing audio guides
- Search and download relaxation and mindfulness apps or online community apps from the NHS apps library

The above tips are taken from the NHS Website (Get help with loneliness - NHS (www.NHS.uk)

Dealing with Pain

Pain is very much a double-edged sword. It can make you, or it can break you. An excellent book from an ex-Navy Seal called David Goggin's called "Can't hurt me" is a case in point. It is impressive what he endured and conquered in the pursuit of his dreams. I can heartily recommend reading this as it can help you believe that you too can endure pain and come through the other side stronger and more resilient, both mentally and physically.

Pain is usually synonymous with being physical, i.e., burning yourself, twisting your ankle, and most of the time, physical pain is relatively temporary, bloody painful, yes, but usually temporary.

However, there are those of us who have long term debilitating, clinical pain. Imagine having to put up with pain every single day. This must get them down enormously, and you can understand why they may get a tad irritable if you hit them with a sarcastic comment. Try and put yourself in their shoes, do what you can to minimize their pain, and don't make it worse FFS.

Mental pain can be even more painful and usually long-lasting, the pain of rejection, loss, and failure. If left to fester, it can grow and severely affect your mental health and everyday life.

If something terrible has happened in our past, we can habitually repeat it over in our minds and base current decisions on this experience. But, whilst we can't change the past, it is unhealthy to relive the bad feelings and anguish day after day, as it brings down your mood and self-worth all the time. But if we use the memory to learn from, and generate a positive outcome for today, and the possible futures, it is definitely worth utilising.

If some issue is really getting you down, creating a load of mental anguish, please, please, talk to a friend about the situation. The old cliché "a problem shared is a problem halved" is really rather true. The more you keep it to yourself, the worse it can get.

I know it may be a difficult subject to divulge to someone else, but it will really help if you can do it. Just talking about it, getting it out there, releases the pressure cooker of anguish.

Our brains are conditioned to protect us, both mentally and physically. It can recognise the danger and automatically engage the good old flight or fight mechanism. However, because we have such a comfortable life these days with no Sabretooth tigers about to rip our heads off, we take it personally and get upset and react to the smallest of events because we aren't conditioned to deal with danger on a daily basis.

This basically means we take everything to heart. We become "offended" at other people's opinions. This is just daft. We are all entitled to our own opinion.

It's up to you whether you can accept that other people have different views to yours. Life is so much more relaxed when you don't get pissed off and angry at every little thing.

It really doesn't matter in the grand scheme of things if your next-door neighbour thinks Sunderland is better than Newcastle. It's just his opinion. It doesn't mean it's right or wrong. It doesn't mean you have to prove Newcastle is the better team.

They might be, but you don't have to rub his face in it.

Depression

This is one subject I have personally not experienced, but I know many friends who have been or are still dealing with depression.

Depression can be such a debilitating condition and can affect every aspect of your life. It is different for everyone. It affects people in different ways, has different triggers, and needs different ways of dealing with it.

There is no magic pill to "cure" depression. Yes, there are many medications out there that can help take the edge off, but they are not the cure, as they don't tackle the core issue causing depression.

Very few people talk openly about their depression, as it still has a negative stigma.

A substantial number of my running buddies say that running has had a massive positive impact on their mental health. They tell me that it really helps reduce the downward spiral of depression and, in a lot of cases, positively helps reduce depression.

So rather than just reading about Depression and then giving my thoughts on it, this chapter will be slightly different. One of my great friends, Michael, has very kindly agreed to share his story about life living with depression:

I worked in the Banking industry since leaving school at the age of 17. With me being profoundly deaf since birth, I did find that I had to concentrate and work smarter and harder in the working environment than my colleagues. I was very proud of myself as I managed to rise to Branch Manager at the Ponteland branch.

The Bank started to go down the Sales route, and although I did well and hit targets, I was working long hours. I was married with 2 very young children and fell ill in 2003, the result of my body being attacked by a virus (Epstein Barr) which causes glandular fever but actually attacked my liver. Suddenly I was exhausted and had no energy to do anything. Even doing small things like cutting the grass was making me very tired.

My confidence and wellbeing took a nosedive. I spent the next few years not being able to do anything and became very reclusive. My moods were very low, and I felt trapped at home, not being able to do things. Some days, I felt like a dark cloud came over me and found it hard to shake off. I was diagnosed with suffering from depression, and my doctor prescribed anti-depressants.

Paranoia set in, with no confidence in myself, and I felt as if people were talking about me when I went out (it was the broken arm syndrome where people can't see what is wrong with you, so they presume you're ok).

Fast forward to 2014, the virus had left my body but left its mark. I was still tired and had no confidence, and was struggling mentally. I decided to get a dog which forced me out of the house. However, If I saw people coming towards me, I would deliberately cross over the road, so I didn't have to interact.

By the end of 2014, I decided to try and get fitter. I did Couch 2 5K and found I enjoyed it. At first, I couldn't run from one lamp post to the next, but over time I managed to run for 30 minutes without stopping. I suddenly found that I loved to go out running and plucked up the courage to enter local races. By the end of the year, I decided to join a local running club to boost my fitness and, more importantly, my mood and confidence. I joined Blyth RC after 1 training session at Churchill playing fields in Whitley Bay. I was so nervous and anxious about meeting new people and thinking I would be the slowest runner there. I was welcomed with open arms and have never looked back.

I am now running marathons and ultras, and although it's still a battle with my depression, the love and support of family and my running friends from BRC have made my life a lot better.

I still have 'bad days', but I can now see the light at the end of the tunnel. I'm not there yet, but I will be.

It is possible to reverse the downward spiral of depression, and exercise is a fantastic way of helping you do so.

If you are really struggling, please seek help, in the UK we are so lucky to have the NHS as a resource, check out their website.

Depression - NHS (www.nhs.uk) gives some really good advice and contact details.

Some Tips on how to cope with depression:

- Stay in touch
- Be more active
- Face your fears
- Don't drink too much alcohol
- Try to eat a healthy diet
- Have a routine

(taken from the Nhs website)

Anxiety

Anxiety is part of life. We get anxious if the bus is late for work, when we are deciding which t-shirt to wear in the morning. We get anxious about not being able to afford the kids Christmas presents, whether or not we will still have a job in 6 months, whether our friend will pull through their cancer treatment.

We all have the odd little doubt, but for some, these niggling doubts can grow and grow until it gets to the point where you begin to doubt everything you do, and even simple, straightforward decisions can be tiring and debilitating.

Anxiety has many triggers, some obvious, some not so much. Our reactions to anxiety can also be very different. For some a temporary feeling, for others, it can last for weeks or even months. Anxiety can bring on panic attacks that can be really rather frightening, shortness of breath, chest pains, and many other effects, which unfortunately makes you feel even more anxious.

Often, anxiety can cause depression and vice versa, and the more we try and ignore it or push it away, the worse it can get.

Thankfully there is lots of good advice out there with many people and services willing and able to help.

The first and most important point is admitting you may have anxiety. This can be very tough. As a bloke, we are supposed to be the strong one, but this only serves to put more pressure on ourselves, causing, you've guessed it, more anxiety.

One of my good friends has very kindly agreed to share their story below:

I am a thirty-odd-year-old (heading rapidly towards my forties) with a family at home. My day job is working as an office manager/jack of all trades in a family run business. I have a large range of hobbies, including interaction with various individuals of varying ages. Most involve some way in which I can be critiqued, compared or observed. Therefore, it can be said that all aspects of my life create opportunities for my anxiety to rear its 'ugly head'. I have 'dealt' with anxiety disorder for over 20 years. Sometimes that's much easier than other times. It took me many, many years to realise that it is perfectly ok to cope better in some situations than others, simply because some situations make me more anxious, which is harder to manage. When dealing with my anxiety, the win for me is not to feel perfectly ok quickly but to feel some form of relief from the anxiety symptoms.

Anxiety for me appears in several forms. Sometimes I struggle to breathe, which can eventually turn into panic attacks (I also have panic disorder), at times I notice myself overthinking (anything and everything, not just what is causing me to be anxious at the time), occasionally I start to hide from the situation, people or places, and often I procrastinate for fear of failing.

About 18 months ago, I realised anxiety plays its part in life. The 'ugly head' I mentioned is sometimes a positive thing as it helps me recognise what I find important and worth 'worrying' about. The key to this anxiety being a positive attribute rather than a negative is shaping how far it takes over me. When I recognise an anxiety indicator early, I try to take a second to think about the positive outcome of what I'm worried about. For example, I am a run leader for our local running club, and as much as I love coaching, I become anxious before most sessions. As I notice it happening, I pause and remind myself it is only a thought. I then think about at least three positive outcomes from completing the session and carry on with those positives as an aim.

Due to my anxiety not appearing the same each time and being far from predictable, I realised that I could not manage this the same way each time. Once I recognise the anxiety symptoms, the first thing I do is remind myself that what makes me anxious is usually a thought. It is not necessarily the activity, person/people or situation but my fear, expectation or memory, but the thoughts I have associated with it. Once this is recognised, I use various coping mechanisms to minimise the impact the anxiety has on my time and feelings.

My 'choice' of mechanism depends on how my anxiety symptoms are materialising. This is mainly because I have found that for me (and that may not be the same for everyone), there is no one way or one answer to 'fix' anxiety. Some anxiety 'attacks' I find myself using distraction. I simply need time to allow the positive outcomes to be processed, so I will jump on the treadmill or play the piano for a short time. If I have found myself trying to hide from an upcoming situation, I tend to put on my headphones and play some music that I know well and will wash over me.

111

This allows me to find positives and refocus my thinking slightly.

When I struggle to breathe, it tends to be due to not recognising other symptoms earlier. These times can require any type of distraction, the most useful being something that regulates breathing, even slightly. I tend to try and sing something familiar (with my headphone in if necessary/possible) or use a familiar meditation video or app. Once I have controlled breathing in some way, I find the positive outcomes.

The main thing I have learnt over the years is that there is no right or wrong answer to moving forward. What works one day may not work the next and, due to the unpredictability of anxiety, the materials or space required may not be available. In these instances, I look for positives in past activities or events as a means of focusing.

As you can see and may have experienced, anxiety can strike at any time, and I think recognising the symptoms of it kicking in early is the key to dealing with it.

How can we help ourselves deal with it?

As it is such a common occurrence, there are many resources out there that can help. A simple search for "what can I do to help deal with anxiety" on your search engine of choice will bring up a multitude of hits.

One of which is this one:

My advice is to try out several different techniques until you
find the one that works for you, but try each one for a decent
amount of time (at least a week) before trying another one.

Choice Time

The **HITS**

Accept that you need help, seek help from a health
professional or peer support group, talk to a friend, don't try
and hide it, read up on the subject, but above all, try different
techniques to try and help yourself

Or

The **SHITS**

Try and "put up with it" become consumed by anxiety, let it
ruin your life

Suicide

As I mentioned at the start of this book, I have lost two friends to suicide, and I really want to do everything I can to help blokes realise that their lives are definitely worth living.

Suicide is a very sensitive topic, and most of the time, we only talk about it when it's too late, i.e., when someone has taken their own life and they are no longer with us. If at all possible, we need to be aware of the warning signs and have the confidence to ask the difficult question: are you contemplating suicide?

Now, when you ask this straight out, it is usually a shock for the person you are asking, and you may just get no, or, of course not, but if you look at their body language, this may give you some clues to whether they are telling you the truth.

If they exhibit some of the following signs:

- A loss of eye contact
- A look of shock
- A change in their expression
- A loss of words and shakiness in their voice

They may have had some suicidal thoughts, and you will need to be ready with a couple more questions

If they admit to feeling suicidal:

Focus on the five significant aspects of their conversations.

- Hope for future/treatment/life – the reasons to stay around
- Specific reasons against taking such extreme actions. – see above
- Ambivalence -not bothered about anything
- Connection to faith

114

- Support systems – Samaritans, health service

If they don't admit to being suicidal, please reassure them that you won't judge them and encourage them to open up if at all possible.

It's also crucial that you don't preach to them, i.e., telling them what they should do, and definitely don't try and play down their feelings or just say they will be fine.

The best thing to do is stay calm, acknowledge their pain and suffering, and above all, listen.

There is some excellent free training is available to help you deal with this very tricky subject, and I implore you to take it, it could help you save someone's life

https://www.zerosuicidealliance.com/training?fbclid=IwAR0EOj4AGx_WvD1yfT2pGpsQOrycYBMsYCm8Q1a-klO-e5xdSeJ_DoRUiIQ

Make them aware of the following support organisations and even ring them for them.

- Samaritans offer a 24-hours a day, 7 days a week support service. Call them FREE on 116 123. You can also email jo@samaritans.org
- Papyrus is a dedicated service for people up to the age of 35 who are worried about how they are feeling or anyone concerned about a young person. You can call the HOPElineUK number on 0800 068 4141, text 07786 209697 or email pat@papyrus-uk.org
- NHS Choices: 24-hour national helpline providing health advice and information. Call them free on 111.
- CALM: National helpline for men to talk about any trouble they feel. Call 0800 58 58 58.

If they continue to discuss suicide and you believe they could go through with it, phone 999 and ask for the contact of the nearest crisis resolution team.

If it is your life that is getting so bad that you can't see any future, and you believe that everyone would be better off without you, and you start contemplating or even planning suicide, this is when you should realise that you really do need some help. And that there is absolutely no shame in asking for help.

If you feel like ending your life, please call 999 or go to A&E and ask for the nearest crisis resolution team's contact. These are teams of mental health care professionals who work with people in severe distress.

I can imagine that you may feel nothing worth living for, but there is really much to live for: Your family, your spouse, your children, your children's children in the future, friendship, love, sunrises, good food, fresh air, mountains.

You would be very much missed, and those left behind suffer for many years, as you can see in the following chapter, a message from the bereaved.

A Message from those Bereaved by suicide

The aftermath of any suicide is horrific. For the parents, the spouse, the kids, the brother, the sister, the best mate. They will have a multitude of emotions, from guilt to sadness and, frequently, anger, especially if it is a widow with children.

The emotional damage of suicide can have a massive effect on those left behind for many years.

I can appreciate that if you are in a suicidal state that you can't see or feel anything other than your own pain, your own crushing feeling of despair. But I implore you to think about what your passing would do to those nearest and dearest to you. They will miss you; they will definitely NOT be better off without you, they want to help you see that life will get better, that you can work through this really tough time.

Most events are temporary in this life, and almost all will not be as bad as we imagine they will be. Unfortunately, our brain has a nasty habit of magnifying those negative thoughts, but if we manage to calm ourselves down and reflect on what is truth and what isn't, we would see that it isn't quite as bad as we first thought.

I have spoken to several ladies who have lost a son, a brother, or a husband, and they are, not unsurprisingly, still affected many years later.

One of those ladies, Poppy, has kindly agreed to share how she and her family have had to come to terms with the loss of her son, Alex. In the hope that by telling his story that she can help make a difference in saving a life:

Growing up, Alex was a very shy young boy...really well behaved, very academically bright. He found it difficult to make friends with the macho sporty boys at school, and many

117

of his friends were girls or quiet academics. But as he grew up, he found a love of extreme sport and extreme clothing. At Uni in Sheffield, he joined the dive team and was into very deep 50m dives. He loved rock climbing and bouldering, a form of free climbing. He cycled at least 100 miles a week. Loved speed. He had no fear button and often had knee jerk reactions to situations that were often his downfall.

After finishing in Sheffield, he decided to start nurse training. He excelled at this and was very passionate about caring for his patients; he hated injustice! In the 2nd year, he went with a friend on an Erasmus program with the Uni to Rovaniemi in Lapland, Finland, to work as a student nurse. Typical Alex was taking part in extreme skiing and had an accident resulting in a severely fractured hip. He was flown home in an air ambulance after extensive surgery. Alex became very depressed as it took 18 months before the fracture healed. His mental health suffered, but we got him some help, and he had just finished his first placement in the hepatology ward. He was exhausted and still in pain, but he visited his girlfriend. A row with her resulted in a fatal overdose. He was only 30 years old.

As the oldest of 4 children, Alex's death had a profound effect on them. They all felt lonely and isolated at times because friends did not understand the pain of grief. Matt felt angry that Alex had taken his own life and guilty that he had not perhaps been there for him ...in fact, they all felt that. Matt also said he was not the big brother, but suddenly he was thrown into that role, feeling he had to protect us all.

One of my daughters suffered terrible anxiety for the first 2 yrs. after losing Alex and read many books on grief to make sense of everything she was feeling.

I did not want to talk about my pain because I wanted to protect them from feeling responsible for looking after me.

Now 4 yrs. on and the initial shock has worn off, it's easier to talk about our grief as a family. We talk about our memories of Alex more now, but all I know is that my thoughts are filled with Alex every day. I try hard not to go into the dark place of thinking, was it my fault, was I not good enough as his mum. I feel so broken I will never be happy again, but you would not know I was carrying such a loss to the untrained eye.

When the vast waves of grief hit, you feel like you are drowning and gasping for air... I am in my car alone, listening to Alex's music, and I let out a deep scream. I find anything that is emotional, in any way, easily reduces me to tears. As time passes, the waves are not so big, and you learn to walk alongside your grief. It's part of you, you can't escape it wherever you go.

If I could have spoken to Alex that night, I would have reminded him how much he was loved, and his problems were not worth dying for, as things would get better with help and a loving family around him. I know Alex well enough to know he would be devastated that he had caused so much pain ....he was a fantastic young man, and we had a great friendship! I miss him every minute of every day, which will never change. Alex was my firstborn baby, my first time at parenting. I feel I have lost part of myself.

I feel very strongly now about young men's mental health, and when I can, I will fight to change gender stereotypes. Men need to talk.

As you can tell from Poppy's story, it is heart-wrenching and devasting for those left behind.

So please, if you are feeling suicidal, reach out to a friend, a parent, a doctor, contact a helpline such as Calm or the Samaritans, phone 999, get yourself to A&E. There are so many people and organisations willing and able to help you realise that your life is very much worth living, that you can get through your current state of despair and that there is absolutely nothing to be ashamed of in asking for help.

- Samaritans offer a 24-hours a day, 7 days a week support service. Call them FREE on 116 123. You can also email jo@samaritans.org
- Papyrus is a dedicated service for people up to the age of 35 who are worried about how they are feeling or anyone concerned about a young person. You can call the HOPElineUK number on 0800 068 4141, text 07786 209697 or email pat@papyrus-uk.org
- NHS Choices: 24-hour national helpline providing health advice and information. Call them free on 111.
- CALM: National helpline for men to talk about any trouble they feel. Call 0800 58 58 58.

You can get through this, you really can, and you will find your way to enjoy life again.

The HITS

The Keys to a Better Life

By believing in yourself and taking care of yourself, your life can be immeasurably more enjoyable and less stressful.

Some of the subjects below intermingle and reinforce each other

Self-Confidence and being at ease with yourself

Right then, this is the big one.

Having confidence in ourselves and our abilities is probably one of the most important aspects to ensuring we can keep our emotions in check and towards the positive end of the spectrum. It also contributes to our general feeling of wellbeing and life satisfaction. It gives us the ability to not dwell on our failures and helps us shrug them off and try again.

Those with little confidence usually have very negative self-talk, don't believe in their actions or abilities, and continually question themselves. This leaves them fearful that they may be wrong and could be "found out". The fear of failure is a constant fixture on their shoulder. The bi-product of this is that it stops them from trying out any new experiences. They will always refer back to when they tried something and failed and use this as a reason not to try again.

I struggled with a lack of confidence throughout my childhood and early adult life until the age of 31. I always tried to please others, always craving praise, which usually never ends well because praise is rarely forthcoming.

I took everything personally. Every slight bit of negativity or sarcasm was like a dagger in my heart. This continued to worsen as the pressure and responsibility of work increased. I even had a couple of panic attacks.

Thankfully my boss at the time, Stephen, saw how much I was struggling with this, and I was allowed to go on a course put forward by my colleague (a lovely lady called Linda) called "How to be Brilliant".

This course turned out to be a huge turning point for me. It made me really look at my life and how I was handling it (or not as the case was).

The Lightbulb Moment

The "How to be Brilliant" course was run by a gent called Michael Heppell. Michael is a best-selling author and public speaker. I was one of about 30 people on a 2-day course named "How to be Brilliant".

I was somewhat unsure and nervous, not really being a confident people person, but I am sure I wasn't the only one in the room with those feelings.

Thankfully Michael knew the type of people that came on this course and dragged us out of our comfort zone with a couple of fun ice-breaking exercises. Michael's boundless enthusiasm, positivity and cheeky chappy persona started chipping away at our inhibitions and doubts in ourselves. It was the start of a full-on 2 days.

We started by looking at where we were in different aspects of our life: Career, health, family, money, relationships, personal development, vision and contribution. We marked ourselves out of 10 on the "wheel of life", the lower the mark highlighting the areas we needed to improve. It was a wake-up call for me, highlighting where I needed to put more effort in.

We touched on many different aspects of life, such as; habits, fears, positivity, limiting beliefs, change.

Michael showed us how to break through our shackles of doubt and our limiting beliefs. Each exercise we did drew us further out of our respective shells, burrowing down to release the real us that had been battered and hidden for many years.

As the day progressed, there was a palpable change in the atmosphere as everyone loosened up, relaxed and started to believe that maybe, just maybe, that there was a better way.

At the end of day one, we were paired up with another buddy from the course, and we were each given a piece of plywood, about a foot square. On this piece of wood, we were encouraged to write down our limiting beliefs, what we most wanted to break free of, what was holding us back, and for me, it was a lack of confidence.

After we had written our limiting belief on the wood in big, bold letters, we were shown how to physically break through the wood. Each of us took turns with our buddy to quite literally smash through our limiting beliefs, and boy did it feel good. I had not felt such joy for many years. Every person in the room broke through the wood. Broke through the shit that we had allowed themselves to be shackled by. The atmosphere in the hotel conference room was euphoric. It was as if the whole room had been charged by a massive bolt of hope and positivity.

Even though we had been going for 11 hours, it felt like a massive slug of adrenalin had been pumped into my system.

I had so many different emotions coursing through my body, happiness, relief, a little bit of anger. It felt like a massive weight had been lifted off my shoulders.

It was such a fantastic feeling to let go of all the shit that had been holding me back for so many years.

I drove home that night a completely different person from the one that had arrived early that morning. So much happier than when I had arrived. I floated home on a wave of positivity and hope for a bright future ahead of me.

By the end of the 2-day course, I finally got it. I finally realised that it doesn't matter what other people think of you, or if they criticise what you do or how you do it. It is merely an opinion. As long as you have done your best, then that is more than good enough.

It was so freeing. It was as if a massive switch had been flipped in my soul. It felt as though I had removed a suit of armour that had been slowly rusting solid around me.

I didn't realise how much I had been holding back, afraid of being my true self, hiding away, fearful of being ridiculed for what I may have said or done.

I finally realised that I didn't need other people's approval to feel good about myself. By finally understanding and believing this, I have become a much more confident, content and happy bloke.

I still count this experience as one of my top 5 life experiences.

To say this turned my life around would be entirely correct. I believe pivotal is the word.

I have never looked back. I love new challenges, I embrace change for the better, I love to learn new skills and meet new people. I am confident and at ease with just being myself.

If someone doesn't like me, or who I am, or what I do, or how I do it, I really couldn't give a shit, as long as I stay true to myself and my values.

This is what confidence and acceptance brings.

Yes, I still have the odd doubt, which is perfectly natural, but I don't let it affect who I am negatively.

We spend far too much time getting defensive or upset when someone questions our ideas, values, and looks. When we have low confidence levels, we always take everything so damn personally. Then the feeling of low self-worth and self-loathing begins knawing away at us.

Does this sound familiar?

Do you really hate Dave in the office because he's constantly sucking up to the boss and putting others down to make himself look good? Yes, I know he's probably a right tit, but who gives a shit? Let him crack on in his sad little game of look at me, look at me, just take pity on him that he has lowered his standards so much that he has become this smary piece of shit.

Try not to let his behaviour wind you up, and please stop yourself from wanting to push his face through the office window. This will only serve to tire you out, become bitter and twisted, and possibly go to jail for ABH, not a good idea. This will not help you get promoted next month or ever.

So the next time this sort of thing happens and you start to feel frustrated or angry:

1) Stop
2) Take a deep breath, no, take 5, calm the hell down.
3) Think, will getting angry make the situation better?
4) I doubt it
5) Take another 5 deep breaths
6) Think about how to not react
7) Yes, I did say that right, how not to react
8) Now, if you absolutely need to say something, just say something non-comital like, mmm, interesting opinion, and just leave it at that and continue what you were doing and ignore the fuckwit.

See, that wasn't so hard, was it? Well, actually, it is. You have to make a concerted effort to do this because the brain goes into fight or flight mode when threatened. The trick is to calm down and say, it's ok, that's just their (probably stupid) opinion.

It's also important not to always feel the need to justify you are right. You don't have to retort, but if you really feel the need, then state your opinion, backed up with known and unquestionable facts (not hearsay), then leave it at that.

Does this make sense? Ok, re-read the above and carry on.

With a decent confidence level, we find it so much easier to just accept the way we are, whether that be of our looks, height, weight, or colour of our hair, and not worry about what other people's opinions are.

The old sentiment of if you can't change it, it is pointless worrying about it is very accurate. Worry brings on doubt which then turns into fear of the unknown....

A positive self-image - you will become who you tell yourself you are

Your self-image is at the core of your wellbeing. With a positive self-image, you can be better prepared to deal with negativity, the occasional failures, the painful losses.

A poor self-image leads to a lack of confidence and self-doubt, creating a rather vicious circle of shit.

When I was 13, my parents encouraged me to join a junior running club. After a few weeks of training, I was put in my first event, a 1500m race at Gateshead Stadium. There were 3 different levels, and the coach decided to put me in the top one, with the really quick lads. I didn't have the confidence at the time to ask why he had done that or raise concerns about whether I was ready for this level. I just mumbled a quick ok and got myself prepared for the race. I came last. I felt humiliated.

I don't remember anything else. I don't remember any positive words from the coach, just the feeling that I had let everyone down. Suffice to say, I did not go back. Still, if I had had a good coach, one who took the time to sit me down and told me why he put me in the top race, what he thought I could have achieved with some hard work, I would have gone back.

As it was, I got nothing, no well done for trying (not that I remember anyway) nothing, humiliation had done its job, and the thought of further embarrassment put me off. I did not go back.

Unfortunately, this was one of many instances of failure, each one nibbling away at my confidence levels. Whilst I should have learned from these events, it wasn't even on my radar to be able to take the positive out of them, wait, hold on, never take the positive out of them, especially as a very insecure teenager,

When we have a piss poor self-image, we can start hating the world and everything in it. We struggle to find even a glimmer of positivity in anything we do.

I used to take criticism and sarcasm very personally, like a personal attack, which basically made me even angrier with myself.

Thankfully, now that I am more aware of my responses and emotions, I can recognise the feelings that criticism can create. I realise it is merely an opinion and acknowledge that I don't need to react negatively. I can shrug it off by either accepting it or ignoring it, both of which are much less stressful.

If someone calls you out on something stupid that you have done, it's so much better to say something like, yup, messed that one up, give a little wry smile and carry on. If you know in your heart that they are right, don't try and argue against them. Put your ego back in its box and move on.

Choice time:

The **HITS**

Ignore the negativity from yourself and others. Just do it, give it everything you have, take confidence from the fact you tried. You never know, you might even enjoy it.

Or

The **SHITS**

Let the bastards get to you. Let them win. Become more depressed and annoyed with yourself, hate yourself and everyone around you,

Positive beliefs - What do you believe in?

When people are asked what they believe in, the answer will probably be God, or I don't believe in God. But this isn't a religion-based question.

- Do you believe that there could be a better way of living?
- Do you believe that there are opportunities out there that could help you feel more content and happier?
- Or do you believe everything is terrible, that the world is unfair, that it always happens to you, that you always have bad luck?
- Do you believe that you will never amount to anything?
- Do you believe that you will never be able to get that dream job?
- Do you believe you will never find "Mr" or "Mrs", right?

Unfortunately, the more you feel the world is against you, the more you will feel down, sad and depressed.

Do you really want to spend the rest of your life moaning about everything, the weather, the price of petrol, the fact that Claire has just been on yet another holiday, that John got the promotion and you didn't?

Just stop it.

Stop it now.

It is self-defeating. The more you do it, the more miserable you will get.

How about doing something more productive, like being determined to be the best you can.

Please do one of either of the following:

1. Accept your current state of affairs and make the best of it, find the positives, make a positive difference

2. Make a plan to change, then actually put this change into practice, i.e., get the hell on with it, do things differently.

Mr Henry Ford once said:

If you always do what you've always done, you will always get what you've always got.

Choice time:

The **HITS**

Believe that you can do it. Believe you can have a happier, more fulfilling life. Look on the bright side of life, appreciate what you have got, enjoy life

or

The **SHITS**

Believe the world is against you. Whinge all the frigging time, be miserable, hate yourself, hate everything

A positive growth mindset & good habits

By the time we hit 18 years old, we already have a set of habits that we have grown into, some good, some not so good.

We aren't even aware of these habits unless we start looking into how we live our lives and how we react to day-to-day situations.

We may have hung around with a group of friends who smoked when we were 14; unfortunately, it's more than likely that if you didn't smoke initially, then you probably soon would if you stayed within this friend group.

Breaking habits is a lot harder than creating them in the first place. Especially if you don't really want to break them, you know you should, but your heart isn't in it. Your chances of you breaking this habit are tiny.

To break a habit does take willpower, but willpower alone is simply not enough. You need a buy-in, a need, a want, a proverbial carrot. But more importantly, it requires action and commitment. It's all too easy to sit back and just keep the status quo. It's much more comfortable. But the longer you continue with a bad habit, like smoking, the longer and harder it is to break it.

One of the best ways of creating a new habit is to attach it to a good habit you already have.

Say you always get up at 6:30, and you need to drink more water each day, so as soon as you get up and go to the kitchen, get a pint of water, down it, repeat, every single day.

The ability to break bad habits, or create better new ones is also linked to your mindset, of which there are two main types, a growth mindset or a fixed mindset.

If you have a growth mindset you will have a good chance of breaking a bad habit. If you have a fixed mindset, you probably don't believe you can change your habit. You will probably say things like, I've always been like this, it's just me, I can't change, I'm too old to change. The more you say this, the more it will become your mantra, your default position, your ball and chain.

Habits and mindest go hand in hand. Each one is intrinsically linked to the other.

When you have a fixed mindset, your habits become more ingrained and harder to break. With a growth mindset, habits can be changed and updated.

The fixed mindset is where we only believe what we have told ourselves. When we tell ourselves the same thing repeatedly, this becomes deep-rooted inside us. It becomes our truth, our being, the values that we refer to in any given situation. This thought and repetition become a habit.

Here's a fixed mindset scenario:

You really think that Macdonald's meals are the best quick takeaway burgers, and you believe Burger king is pants.

You start chatting to a new colleague at work, John, and he thinks that Burger King is the business and that Maccy D's is rank.

Now you start to get wound up about this. What does John know? He must be an idiot, I don't like John, and at work, you continue to be annoyed with John and start picking up on other things you don't like about him. He has coffee with 3 sugars! not just 1 like me.

With a fixed mindset, we compare other people's thoughts and ideas to our own habits and values, and if they disagree with us, it winds us up. We get annoyed because it makes us question our own values. It makes you question whether you are right.

We don't like this.

The next stage is when we try and convince John that our preference is better, pointing out all the reasons why, and he starts getting annoyed and argues his case. You stop talking at work together because your views are so different, and now you shun each other at work. You even start bad-mouthing him, as does he about you, and it spirals out of control into a completely pointless, energy-sapping, negative situation.

This happens all the time.

It's all down to our pride and ego, and this is about a relatively minor point, but it festers, it grows, it gets worse.

Does this sound familiar? Can you see some of your own traits in this example?

There is another way.

The growth Mindset.

In this same situation, a person with a growth mindset would take on board John's point of view, his opinion, and say, yeah, I can see why he likes his way better, but I still enjoy my way, but yours is not "better", neither is his. It's just different!

It's just a different opinion, and that's ok. That's fine and completely natural. We are all different, so why should we expect other people to have a similar opinion! It's mad!

When we can accept another person's opinion, it makes life so much more agreeable, calm and relaxed. You don't have to agree with them or try and prove your opinion is "right" and theirs is "wrong". Just chill the hell out and agree to disagree.

To accept other people's opinions for what they are (just opinions) is definitely the way forward. They are not personally attacking you. They are just voicing their thoughts based on their value set. Please don't feel you have to defend your value set "against" another person.

When you have two individuals with a strong, fixed mindset and many differing opinions, it's a recipe for disaster.

There is so much shit that goes around this world with certain individuals trying to enforce their way of thinking onto others and slinging muck on any other conflicting opinion. Let's take a certain American, Mr Orange man. He has such a fixed mindset he can't take even the slightest difference of opinion and goes all out and attacks anyone that dares to question him. He's a rather sad, sad man and a very dangerous one. He is not interested in anyone but himself. The whole presidency has been a massive ego trip for him, a popularity contest. He is continually praising himself, constantly putting down others. I have had shits with better morals. Can you tell I don't like him? but that's just my opinion ☺

The benefits of a growth mindset are many. Here are two of the most important ones:

Accept that attaining perfection is nigh on impossible

Those in a fixed mindset may reach for the stars, but when they fail and realise that it may not be possible to get there, they continually beat themselves up for "not being good enough" or "too stupid".

Those with a flexible growth mindset will recognise that failing is part of learning, a chance to increase their knowledge, a chance to do it better next time.

Getting out of our comfort zone

This is directly linked to our mindset, confidence levels, belief structure, and our values.

As we age, we become more set in our ways. The more set in our ways we are, the more likely we will push back when change is pushed onto us. We will probably not like to try out new things, different foods, different places for holidays etc.

I believe there are three major types of people:

- Optimists,
- Pessimists
- Dontgiveashits.

Optimists are hopeful souls, always looking on the bright side of life, usually turning setbacks into positives. An optimistic person will take the best out of any situation and enjoy it the best they can.

Pessimists are a little afraid of the world, always fearful of what might happen IF so and so does this, IF it rains tomorrow, IF they lose their job. They go from one worst-case scenario to another, living in a constant state of nervousness about what could happen, and it is very rarely an optimistic scenario. Even if they won the lottery, they would be worrying about what to do with the money, how much to give to their family & friends, etc.

Dontgiveashits are pessimists who have more or less given up. They are just so pissed off with absolutely everything that they don't give a shit, not about their families, friends, situation, but worst of all themselves. They have lost the will or inclination to look at the bright side of life. They have become so used to their negative viewpoint on the world and everyone that there is almost no way a tiny glimmer of hope can get through to them, unless someone can help them to open their eyes to hope.

To be an optimist, you need to be pretty sure and confident in who you are, i.e., accepting that you and the world are not perfect. There are many possibilities to make tiny perfect moments in time, sometimes unexpectedly (the best kind) and other times through a combination of being in the right place at the right time. But nothing is perfect for long, which is why we need to enjoy each and every little victory

I believe we are all a little scared and unsure of ourselves. Some of us just handle it or hide it better than others. Some use it to push us forward and open ourselves to new experiences. Others go in the opposite direction, trying less and less new things, becoming more unsure of themselves, and unwilling to take even the slightest risk.

It comes back to believing in ourselves and a willingness to take a little leap into the unknown. Not to overthink or care about the potential of failure. Just give it a go, try your best, that's it.

Don't think, just do.

You may surprise yourself with how much you can achieve.

Positive affirmations and visualisation

Another technique that I have found helpful and use regularly is positive affirmations and visualisations.

These are used to prime your brain to deal with stressful or difficult situations.

For instance, before an interview, you can get rather uptight and nervous. To help quell your nerves, sit quietly, close your eyes, and then visualise yourself walking calmly into the interview room, meeting whoever is in there with a confident greeting. Then picture your upright and attentive posture, with a smile on your face and see yourself answering the questions efficiently.

Your brain thinks this is an actual event, so that when it does happen, it refers to this visualisation, thus helping you to remain calm.

From an affirmation point of view, I would suggest the following: I would get to the interview a little early. If you travel by car, sit quietly in the driver's seat, look in the vanity mirror, and repeat 10 times, I can do this while taking big deep breaths. Ideally, do this out loud. This calms you down and gets you into a positive mindset for the interview.

A friend of mine used to have a happy list when he was applying for jobs, to which he would look at in the waiting room to help get into a happy, smiley place.

As a runner, I use the following affirmation when I start to struggle at the end of a race; looking good, feeling great. I repeat this for at least a minute, usually out loud, as you get more benefit. This achieves two important goals:

1) It helps you ignore the negative thoughts coming from your body (which is trying to convince your brain that you need to slow or stop)

2) It also tricks your brain into thinking you are looking good and feeling great so that you can keep running at your current pace and push through the fatigue.

This may sound silly, but I use it regularly. It works.

Effective Communication (or lack of)

Most of us really struggle with this one. The emphasis here is on the word "effective".

There are many different mediums to communicate through; our voice, what we say and how we say it, the written word, facial expression, body language, posture, touch (i.e., a handshake), and our actions, and conversely, our inactions.

A lot of our communication methods are misinterpreted. Email is probably the worst one for this. If you are short and to the point, it can come across as rude and insensitive.

Without communication, we would never get anything done. We wouldn't be able to express our feelings, hopes, and fears. We would not fully understand or confirm instructions nor react accordingly to the signals and signs given by another person.

To communicate effectively, we need to be mindful of how we express our needs and opinions. We need to recognise and take on board the signs given out by the person we are speaking with.

We have a nasty habit of being so caught up in what we want to get across that we don't notice the other person's reactions and just mindlessly continue to bleat on and on and on.

Some of us say too much, some of us don't say enough, most of us don't listen properly.

We rarely stop and think about what we are about to say. We just blurt it out, then have to deal with the consequences.

When we have a "discussion", or shall I say "argument". Our emotional state plays a massive part in how we communicate. If you are really wound up before you open your mouth, you are already screwed.

When you are angry or frustrated or scared, your brain moves into fight or flight mode yet again, circumnavigating all reason, logic and common sense. This is why arguments can end in violence or tears as our logical brain has been completely ignored, and the brain's emotional side goes into overdrive.

This never ends well. It just makes everything a whole lot worse.

If you need to say something really important, my advice is to think it over before speaking out loud, consider the following points

- Is it vital to say this now?
- What do you hope to achieve by saying this?
- Will it hurt the other person?
- Is it the truth?
- Is it a statement based on what someone else has said or told you?
- Think about it from the other person's point of view
- Is the other person having a good day? Ask them how they are doing first, then let them talk first

Unless you have considered the points above, I would stop and think again before opening your mouth.

We are usually far too reactive, our ego gets hurt, someone is questioning what we hold to be true, and we usually can't handle this. We feel the need to justify ourselves, to tell our side of the story. Because if we can't or won't accept the other person's point of view, we can see that as a failure on our side. But this simply isn't true.

The reason is: **We are, all, Different.**

- We think differently
- We act differently
- We have different things that wind us up
- We have different values
- We have different habits
- We have experienced different things in our lives
- We believe in different things
- We like different things
- We dislike different things
- We get annoyed by different things
- We enjoy different things
- We have different backgrounds
- We have different expectations
- We have different hopes and dreams

And this is why we can find it so hard to communicate.

Unless we have some common ground, we can really struggle to appreciate someone else's point of view. If we really hold dear to our own beliefs, our own little world, it doesn't matter what the facts are, or what someone else has experienced, or what someone else believes, we just dig our heels in even more to try and prove we are right and everyone else is wrong.

So how do we help ourselves and everyone around us?

- We need empathy – try and understand and feel what the other person could be going through
- We need patience – stop and think before reacting,
- We need acceptance of other people's points of view – yes, they are allowed to have one
- We need to chill the hell out

Choice time:

The **HITS**

Become a more considerate and empathic person by acknowledging someone else's point of view

or

The **SHITS**

Always try and prove you are right, get angry and stressed out, act like a bit of a dick.

Listen, yes you

The flip side to talking is obviously the listening part; this is even more important.

When someone talks to us, it's only right that we treat them with respect and actually listen to what they have to say. Rather than talking over them, or just formulating what we want to say as a reply without really giving a damn about what they are saying.

Sometimes we are so eager to get our point of view across that we don't even hear the question properly, or we hear it, but we hear what we want to hear. But that's not listening.

I know that it can be challenging, especially if the person speaking is droning on about the same subject again and again, but try and understand why they are doing that.

They might be talking complete bollocks, but it's respectful to allow them to try and communicate their feelings, plans, hopes and fears. By giving someone the space to talk encourages them to trust you and open up even more. Everyone wants to be heard. They just want their point of view to be acknowledged.

Politicians don't appear to listen very well. They are a nightmare for answering questions, especially when asked a difficult question. They usually respond with a reply as if they were asked an entirely different question. I.e., they choose not to hear, or ignore altogether what is actually being asked. This could be so that they don't have to answer the original question, allowing them to get their own agenda across.

By listening effectively, we can communicate more effectively.

If we don't make an effort to listen appropriately, this shows a lack of respect. It's really rather rude. It makes the other person think, "why am I bothering even talking?"

Direct questioning + Focussed listening = effective communication

The old adage of a problem shared is a problem halved is another reason why the ability to listen is so damn important. If we notice one of our friends is a little down or not their usual self, please ask them how they are doing. How's work, life at home? We really need to make an effort to get our friends to open up about what is bothering them, what is really bugging them, because if we don't, they usually just bottle up their frustration.

With no outlet, with no voice of reason to retort against their inner voice, there is no respite from the feelings of self-doubt and insecurity. This can really bring them down and can lead to some very negative thoughts.

As friends, we always try to help, to give our opinion on how we would solve the issue, but we aren't in the same position, we are not the same person, so we can't really advise how they should react.

Sometimes it's more than enough to just listen, nod, be empathic, don't judge, but give them your full attention and give them the respect they deserve.

When they have got it off their chest, maybe ask if they would like some suggestions on how to deal with it or, even better, encourage them to narrow down the problem themselves so that they can work it out. This has a much better chance of working. Simply encourage them. Sometimes that's more than enough.

The Control Conundrum

When we feel in control, we are more at peace with ourselves. We are more relaxed, happier.

When we are not in control, it makes us uneasy, nervous, and dependent on the situation, rather stressed.

We have a tendency to overthink things and feel we don't have enough control.

As of January 2021, we were in another covid lockdown in the UK. We were not in control of what we could and couldn't do. This was really rather frustrating. Sometimes we are somewhat selfish, only thinking about how it affects us and how we feel. Still, by looking at the bigger picture, i.e., saving lives, we needed to accept that specific rules and recommendations should be followed.

There are day-to-day occurrences out of our control, the car breaks down, or the boss loads you with yet another project with an impossible deadline.

Again, dependent on our state of mind at that particular moment, it can make our current situation a whole lot worse.

We can't predict the future, but it's up to us to decide how we handle the shit that arrives at our doorstep.

We can let it get to us, or we can realise that it isn't in our control and just deal with it the best we can.

We put a lot of pressure on ourselves these days to cram loads of stuff into our day, sometimes it is necessary. But when we don't manage to do absolutely everything, we can beat ourselves up, and the negative voices start creeping in, you're useless, you're not good enough, anyone could do this.

This can really stress us out, especially when it happens day after day.

There are a few things to help you deal with this, firstly don't take too much on, learn to say: "sorry I have not got enough time to do that today" or a simple "no", take some of the pressure off yourself, be kind to yourself.

Secondly, if it is out of your control, go easy on yourself. It's not your fault. Just do your best. That is enough, more than enough.

Stop trying to be perfect. It's an impossible task; striving for perfection and not attaining it only serves to stress you out even more!

To summarise, work with what you can control to build your confidence and feel good about yourself. Don't stress about what you can't control. It will only make you feel like shit.

CHOICE TIME

The **HITS**

Accept that you can't control everything, don't get upset or stress yourself out about things out of your control.

OR

The **SHITS**

Try and control everything. Stress yourself out massively when you can't. Get really anxious about what might happen, lose confidence, get upset over tiny little things far too quickly.

Optimism

Optimism is the Yang of Pessimisms Yin.

Optimism is a positive state of mind, always looking at the bright side of life and what it can bring.

Pessimism is expecting everything to be shit, to not work out, to fail. But if we expect everything to fail, then there is a much higher percentage of this happening, with very little chance of success.

When we expect things to go wrong and they do so, it prolongs the agony, with only the sad and depressing knowledge that we were right about how nothing goes our way. This only reinforces the feeling of uselessness, sadness and dejection.

Even when things turn out ok, pessimists never take joy in this, or struggle to take comfort from the fact that everything turned out ok because it doesn't fit in with their usual way of thinking.

Whereas if we put ourselves in a positive frame of mind and believe that things usually turn out ok, we can keep our spirits high. Even if they don't turn out as we expected, we can handle it because that's just life.

As Eric Idle sang in the Life of Brian, "Always look on the bright side of life" because it makes life so much more relaxing, happy and enjoyable. If you can't control the outcome of any given event, stop stressing about it all the time, stop worrying about all the negative what-ifs. It's pointless.

So how about you try and throw caution to the wind, stop moaning, stop blaming the world for your problems, just go with the flow, chill the hell out and enjoy life!

In Search of Happiness

This is like the search for the holy grail. It's almost an impossible dream to attain and keep your state of happiness.

Most people strive for happiness, but a lot of people say that they have to get something first, then they will be happy, but this usually doesn't happen on two counts

- They don't achieve their happiness goal, i.e., it's too complicated or challenging, and they give up and find another goal instead, which they will also fail to achieve.
- They finally achieve their goal but soon find themselves unhappy and look for a new goal that will make them happy

Happiness is usually seen as a destination, but it's not. It's about making the most of the journey to enable a general feeling of contentment and happiness.

We have a nasty habit of blaming everything and everyone around us for the state of our unhappiness.

Are you unhappy because Sheila got the promotion and you didn't? Really? Did you deserve it? have you worked as hard as Sheila? Have you got into work early and left late on numerous occasions? Have you supported the business, made sacrifices to get the job done? Or is it just because you have been there longer than Sheila, that you thought you should get it?

We are our own worst enemy when it comes to happiness. We like to find excuses, why it's someone else's fault, so we don't have to face reality.

If we actually take a step back and look at ourselves and our situation, we would realise it's up to us to decide how we react.

Giving something back & gratitude

This isn't something we think about regularly. Christmas day doesn't count!

In our busy, hectic, fraught lives, we always seem to focus on the negatives, the car didn't start, and you were late for work, the boss was angry, and thus your whole day was ruined. No, it wasn't. You let one thing out of your control affect your entire day. Sometimes we allow bad feelings from one day to roll into the next. If we do this all the time, we end up whingeing all the time, which is not good for you or the people around you, as you will also bring their mood down.

We have also got into the habit of expecting everything to be perfect. So, when something bad happens, we don't handle it very well.

Life is not perfect.

If you expect to have the perfect job with the perfect partner and the perfect house, you will be well pissed off most of the time because perfection is unachievable for any sustained length of time. It's can also be stressful and frustrating, trying to be perfect.

Life is all about ups and downs. The downs make you more grateful for the ups!

This is where gratitude comes in. If you have a house, a job, and a partner, then you should be grateful. Many people are living rough on the streets with one pair of clothes and a cardboard box to live in. They are thankful for a coffee and a dry place to sleep. Would you like to swap places with them? In one way, we should try a night on the streets, to appreciate what we do have.

So, the next time you start feeling sorry for yourself or annoyed that you can't afford a new car this year, just be thankful that you have one.

We are pretty materialistic these days. We all want the latest phone, the trendiest clothes, the most followers on Instagram.

It's all me, me, me.

We work hard to have stuff, we work harder to get more stuff, we don't see our kids during the week because we are chasing the next big bonus. We lose sight of what is really important, our kids, our wife, our health. We only really notice when it's too late when we have a heart attack or get home to an empty house because the missus has had enough and left.

We spend far too much time on our phones these days. Continually scrolling to see who is up to what and where. We are continuously comparing ourselves to others, trying to be like them. We really need to put our phones down and look around at what we have actually got.

The number of times I see parents with their kids at a playground, just sitting on a bench with their head in their phones, not engaging with their kids, looking at yet another pointless video clip on YouTube, or liking yet another post of that twat from Towie.

How often do you get out of the house, leave your phone in your pocket, drive to a country park and just have a gentle walk with the missus and the dog? Our brains need time to relax and chill out, it gives them time to compute the latest inputs in our subconscious, and then develop a possible solution, with virtually no conscious effort from yourself.

So how do we extract ourselves from the constant chatter from social media? You know the answer; just put the fucking phone down. It distracts us at work, at home, even when we are out with our mates, we sit there laughing to ourselves rather than engaging with our friends.

By thinking of others, giving something back rather than expecting something all the time is the way forward. From the smallest of things like holding a door open for someone, or letting a car out of a side street, to ringing a mate that you haven't spoken to for ages just for a chat to see how they are. Random acts of kindness (RAOK) are epic, the spur of the moment action that can make such a difference to someone's day.

Appreciation

Sometimes we are so caught up in our own little world, with its day-to-day stresses, that we rarely sit back and appreciate what we have achieved or enjoyed that day. We have a natural tendency to focus on the negative, but when we do this, we live in a state of negativity. Put another way, if you live and play in shit, you will always smell of it, and after a while, all you can see is shit.

Appreciating what we have, rather than beating ourselves up for what we don't have, should make us realise how lucky we actually are.

One of my friends suggests that the following should be done once a day (to help remind myself to do it, I set the alarm on my phone at 9pm each day):

- Recount 3 good things that happened today – e.g., an enjoyable catch up with a mate, completing a task at work, received a compliment
- Name 3 things that you are grateful for today – e.g., being able to go for a run, have a job (even if it is a challenge sometimes), having a good mate to talk to.
- Think of 1 positive thing you will aim for tomorrow, e.g., to accept that not everything will exactly go to plan, but to go with the flow and make the best of it.

This makes you focus on the positives. It should help make you feel better about yourself and more at ease with the world. It also shuts up your head's negative voice for a little while.

It is time to live your life. It's something to be experienced and enjoyed, not endured and hated.

It saddens and disappoints me when someone is whingeing about something small and inconsequential. Our great grandparents lived through a time of real hardship and stress. Living through wartime must have been ridiculously difficult with all of the uncertainty, pain, and outright terror

Nowadays, we are so self-righteous about our "rights" and how "tough" things are. Are they bollocks? Most of us have no real sense of what real hardship really is. We should be grateful for the simple things in life, access to clean water, a roof over our head, a warm house, food on the table.

CHOICE TIME

The **HITS**

Appreciate what you have and accept that other people have different opinions to yours, stay calm and carry on.

OR

The **SHITS**

Be an entitled, selfish prick. Think that the world deserves to give you what you want.

The **Tips**

- Be grateful for what you have got.
- Take a proverbial chill pill
- Don't be a dick.

Perspective & Attitude

The definition of perspective: a particular attitude towards, or way of regarding something (e.g., another person); a point of view.

As we are all different, each of us has a different perspective on life, with a unique way of seeing the world.

If you are standing next to someone and you watch the same event, you may have a completely different take on the situation, as you will see it through the eyes of your own values and experiences.

There is no right or wrong reaction or thought generated from an event. It is merely that persons take on a unique situation.

Through our own "virtual glasses", we see entirely different things. We draw vastly different opinions, based upon our individual past experiences.

Unfortunately, we have a tendency to judge other people for a different point of view, rather than accept they are allowed to see things from their own unique perspective.

We don't know what shit the other person has been through in their life to bring them to this point, so just accept that they will have a different view of things.

The even worse thing that can then stem from a differing perspective is anger. We take it personally when someone else dares to have a different opinion from our own. We let our ego take over, and we can get a bit nasty and try and put down the other person's opinion. We belittle their thoughts, all just to justify our own position.

It's ok to question and try to understand why they think like that (but in a nice way!), but then they could take this the wrong way, i.e., as a personal attack on their opinion, and then off we go, argument time.

If we just accept other people and their opinions for what they are, i.e., opinions. Then both parties would get a lot less stressed and angry.

Even if you really don't agree with what someone else is saying, it isn't a personal attack on you. It is just their fucking opinion. Stop getting upset or angry. Just let it go, just change the subject and talk about something else. It's a lot better for everyone.

Another side to perspective is attitude. Some people see, or even seek out, the negative in any given situation to find problems, a reason not to do something.

This is usually based on their past experiences and unwillingness to try something different from how they would typically do something. I believe it is a mix of a fixed mindset and a lack of confidence.

They may worry about what may happen, anticipate danger around every corner, try and control every situation to reduce or even remove the uncomfortable or anxious feelings that stepping outside of their fixed comfort zone may entail.

Step out of your comfort zone, realise that you can do more than you think you can, to realise that you can take on board another way of doing things, that you can try out a different technique, consider an alternative option.

Cliché time "variety is the spice of life" it's not wrong.

You can do this.

Random Acts of Kindness (RAOK)

I love doing Raok's for others. The look of pleasant surprise on the other persons face is simply priceless. A fantastic by-product of carrying out a RAOK is that you usually get a lovely warm fuzzy feeling in return.

Let me tell you about one RAOK experience of mine:

I was running in the countryside with my good running buddy Pete, on a disused railway line in Durham. It's quite a popular little track with multitudes of walkers, dogs, bikers, and fellow runners all enjoying the countryside. We were on our way back towards our start point, and I noticed a lady with a couple of dogs. As a dog owner myself, I notice dogs whenever I am out and about. They always make me smile, well, almost always, not so much when they start barking and chasing me whilst running.

Anyway, I run past the lady and her dogs, and I notice her carrying a rather substantial black bag full of shit. My mate and I run this route fairly frequently, and as I passed her, I realised that there weren't any bins in the direction she was going for a few miles, and I knew there was one a couple of hundred meters ahead of me in my direction.

So, after thinking about this for a second, I stopped running, turned around, and tried to catch the lady's attention, "excuse me ", she looked up to see a random, rather sweaty bloke, trying to get her attention, I then said, "let me take that bag for you".

She looked somewhat puzzled. I could see it passing across her face, with the expression WTF probably running through her mind. I carried on unperturbed, and I repeated, "let me take that bag for you," then added, "there are no bins for at least a couple of miles, and I know there is one a couple of hundred meters in my direction".

A raft of emotions passed across her face, the first one of relief that I wasn't a complete nutter, then one of gratefulness and then a big embarrassed smile came creeping across her features, "really? are you sure? " She tentatively asked, "yeah, no worries, I am a dog owner myself and know how much of a pain it is to carry around a bag of shit around for miles".

I then planted the biggest fuck-off smile on my face and gently took it out of her hand. She gave me a timid little smile, thanked me again, and then off I went to catch up with my mate and towards the bin to dispose of said bag of shit.

Now, not only am I feeling good about doing a good deed what happened next really made my day:

As we approached the bin, another group of runners approached us, and here I was carrying a bag of shit and running without a dog. Feeling a tad self-conscious, I gave a hearty good morning and said cheerfully, "it's not mine!" to which my running mate Pete retorted within a second with the fantastic words "it isn't mine either" this made me laugh out loud. I continued to laugh and smile for the next ten minutes. It was such great timing and sharp that it really tickled me.

This two-minute interaction, stemming from a small random act of kindness, really made my day, a moment of genuine light-heartedness at nobodies' expense but our own.

So, you can see what can be a fantastic, uplifting by-product of a small act of kindness. You may not be thanked for it all the time, but whilst it may be a tad rude when this happens, the other person may be having an awful day, so the act of doing it is still very pertinent.

It can really make a positive difference to someone's day by carrying out the simple act of giving, a moment of kindness, or a helping hand.

The feeling of wellbeing also lasts longer than the actual deed, a gift that keeps giving, for both yourself and the recipient, all by carrying out a simple random act of kindness. It's like a ray of sunshine obliterating a cloud.

Giving and helping others allows us to stop worrying about our own shit, even if just for a little while.

Meditation & its benefits

For a few years now, I have heard many good things about how meditation can help you deal with life's daily stresses. My initial thought was, "what a load of bollocks", but a good friend of mine whose opinion I value also extolled the virtues of it. So, I thought it was about time that I should give it a go.

First things first, you don't need any candles, or incense or say ommmmmmm, unless you really want to. All you need is a comfy chair, a quiet place and at least 5/10 mins.

To help you meditate, there are several meditation apps. Most of them are free for the basics, then they want your dosh. Another way is to search on YouTube, try CALM. It has nice soothing background noise then an American bird starts talking about useful (mostly) stuff.

But it's mainly about just trying to focus on your breath, how it enters and leaves your body. Just the simple act of counting in and out just relaxes and calms the brain. It's perfectly natural for thoughts to swirl around. The trick is not to engage with them, just be aware of them, then refocus on your breath, in and out, in and out.

There is no right way of doing meditation, or as I call it, sitting calmly, trying not to get distracted. It does take practice and patience, but you will find it more natural as time goes by. If you can persevere and focus on your breathing, just once a day for 5/10 mins, then you should see the benefits, namely:

The benefits of meditation are:

- Can help control Anxiety
- Can reduce stress levels
- Can improve the quality of your sleep
- Can increase your attention span
- Enhances self-Awareness
- Promotes good emotional health

As you find yourself being run ragged, with loads of thoughts rushing around your brain, just stop, take five minutes in a quiet place and simply breathe in and out. It is definitely worth giving it a go.

Try and get into the habit of doing it daily, and you should find yourself a lot calmer and hopefully less inclined to bite someone's head off if they say something you disagree with.

Try it.

It works.

Acceptance

This is another important one with two sides to it.

There is acceptance of ourselves and the acceptance of others.

I think the tougher of the two is the acceptance of ourselves. But once we come to terms with the way we look and are content with what we have rather than chasing a distant horizon, we can finally relax and be happy. By being grateful for what we have, rather than fretting about what other people have and their opinions of us.

This state of mind is heavily linked to our self-image and confidence. If we lack these two aspects, we usually beat ourselves up a lot. We worry so much about what others think of us that we try to become something we are not. We try too hard, we pick faults with ourselves, we try and project a "perfect" image of confidence when in reality you may be feeling like shit or close in on yourself and not interact with other people. Neither situation is healthy.

So, what can you do to help you accept who you are?

Firstly, try not to take any negative comments personally. They are just opinions. I am sure those people slinging insults or put-downs are not perfect themselves. They are probably feeling just as unsure of themselves. Still, their way of handling it is to put down others just so that they can feel superior, which is a bit sick and twisted if you ask me, but that's just my opinion.

So, stand up straight, look em in the eye, then just walk away. They are not worth any of your time or attention. I wouldn't waste the steam off your piss on them.

Their opinion doesn't matter. Really, it doesn't.

Don't be afraid to be who you are or who you want to be. It's time to say sod it and just go for it, so much better than feeling belittled and depressed.

The flip side of the acceptance coin is the acceptance of others.

To repeat, we are all different. We have differing points of view, values, tastes, and backgrounds. Please try and accept it when someone has an outlook on life that is different from yours! You don't need to justify your version of life or your thoughts, nor should you try and convince them they are wrong. They are not wrong!!! They just have a different opinion.

You don't have to agree with them, just accept their point of view, you might think they are talking complete bollocks, but that's ok, but please don't say it out loud? Just give a non-committal shrug or a "ahhh, really?"

They are not attacking you personally, so don't react as if they are. Try not to react negatively at all. It serves no purpose other than to get each other riled up. You can say things like "I can see where you are coming from" and "really? I haven't heard that before".

This is rather hard to do, but you will get there with practice, and you will finally manage to keep your ego in check. When it's your turn to tell them your thoughts, they will probably try and justify their position/point of view, but don't react; they just act on their ego's.

Forgiveness

There are two aspects of forgiveness, firstly the obvious one, forgiveness to others. The other one that we don't really think about is forgiveness for ourselves.

We are human. We mess up on a regular basis, daily, in fact. But that's completely normal. Sometimes we try something out, and it doesn't work. Sometimes we make a mistake, but that's ok.

We seem to get angry at ourselves when we have made a mistake, we start doubting ourselves and our capabilities, we think we are stupid, which makes us wary of trying new things.

The worst thing is when we blame others for this, we try and divert our feelings of embarrassment from ourselves and take it out on our nearest and dearest.

The much less stressful route is to accept that we make mistakes and admit them to ourselves and others, and if it is your fault, say sorry FFS. Say sorry and move on. Learn from it, try not to do it again, change how you do things to get a better result next time.

The forgiveness of others isn't all that easy either. It is one of the hardest things to do. Whether it's forgiving something relatively inconsequential like a harsh word or a lot more severe like physical or mental abuse of the past.

If we continue to hold onto the pain of our past and relive it constantly, we are still under the control of what happened. It still affects us. But if we can accept that it happened and try and forgive it/them, we can finally start to move forward.

When we stop beating ourselves up, we can stop hating ourselves. We can put the past demons to bed and leave them there. Then we can move forward and start enjoying life.

Don't be a Dick

Sometimes we can act like a bit of a dick, but none of us are good when it comes to admitting this. Most of the time, it happens when we are frustrated or stressed, but some blokes are arrogant, some just lifelong dickheads.

I believe there are many types of dickhead, but I will focus on the main two major types:

The reactive dickhead, and the proactive dickhead.

Unfortunately, when you have the traits of one, you can probably guarantee that you will also have the other.

We can all lose our rag sometimes, whether it's because someone cut us up on the motorway or pushed into a queue in front of us, or someone said something that we really thought was absolute bollocks. But unless it's a life-or-death situation, is it really worth getting all worked up about?

We get so mad at the stupidest little things that wind us up, and we then proceed to make a huge deal about it. This just causes a massive amount of stress and anger, usually for very little reason whatsoever.

We get mad about the things we can't change, the weather, the fact that most politicians are arseholes that can't and won't answer a simple question.

This is such a waste of our time and energy.

So rather than rise to the annoying person or event, just ignore it, simply say a quiet" dickhead" in your head, smile and carry on.

So that takes care of the reactionary dickhead behaviour.

The harder (no pun intended) habit to break is to stop being a proactive dickhead.

A proactive dickhead will provoke an argument, say something to someone to get a reaction, and force their point across or put your opinion down. I believe they do this to feel smug and superior, utterly oblivious to others' feelings or wellbeing. They don't even think about how their words could affect the other person. They couldn't give a shit.

Are you one of those people that likes to wind other people up, just for shits and giggles? The only time I think this is acceptable if you are really good mates with the other person and that they do the same to you, "friendly banter". However, if it is to someone you don't really know, please stop doing this.

Yes, you may get a few laughs from your other friends or colleagues, but at what cost? Do you know what that particular person is going through at that moment in time? Probably not? Do you know that his wife left him this morning for another bloke? Probably not. Could this "piss-taking" be the last straw for him? Let's hope not.

I have never thought it funny to wind someone up as I have been on the receiving side of this and know how it affected me, pretty badly.

Some people like to wind up their significant other just because they have pissed them off, rather than dealing with it like an adult. No, they make things worse. Well done, not.

Please, please, please try and put yourself in the other person's shoes before you have a go at them. Try and understand why they act as they do, rather than taking it personally and lashing out.

12 GOLDEN RULES (daily)

1) Accept yourself for who you are

2) Understand and accept that everyone is different

3) Be patient

4) Be nice to yourself

5) Do something nice for someone else – RAOK

6) Eat sensibly, everything in balance and moderation

7) Drink 2.5 litres of water each day

8) Try and get at least 7 hours of sleep each night

9) Exercise at least 30 mins each day

10) Be thankful and appreciative for what you have

11) Count to 10 and think before reacting/opening your mouth

12) Don't be a dick

The important bit – over to you.

Hopefully, some of the points that I have brought up in this book have resonated with you. I hope you can see a glimmer of possibility that you could have a more enjoyable, less stressful life.

But to be able to experience this new way of living, you need to want it. If it's something you know you should be doing, then get the hell on with it and just do it, don't just talk about it, stop making excuses, stop finding other things to do so that you don't do it.

Sometimes you need to feel the pain of not doing something. It needs to get that bad that you have no option than to change what and how you do things. But how about you take a good hard look in the mirror and do something before it gets unbearable? If it isn't painful enough, you probably won't change anything. You will just stay in your comfort zone, pottering along in life without any real purpose. Then before you know it, you will be 70 years old and have shit loads of regrets, starting with the words, I wish I..., and, If only I...

But if you want to do something about it and want to be able to have the confidence to try new things to enjoy your life, you will need to make a plan and a commitment together with some tangible and pretty realistic goals.

Life really is an opportunity. It's the reason why we are here.

So, it's down to you. It really is.

Changing the way you deal with things that happen in your life can be difficult, but if you aren't happy with the way things are going at the minute and want something more from life, you have to do something differently.

Some opportunities land on us as if by magic. Some could say karma. These can be both good or not so good but both give us opportunities to learn and grow.

The flip side is the creation of our own opportunities. The trick is to put our minds into the correct state to make the most of them and give them a go to make them into reality, i.e., optimism and curiosity.

Please try to let go of your inhibitions, the fear of failure, the overthinking, and just follow your initial gut feeling and give it a go. The important thing is the act of trying. Sometimes it doesn't work out. Sometimes it does. Sometimes it works out differently than you expected, but each outcome still moves you forward. You will have learned something as a result.

If you give it your best shot, put your heart and soul into it, you can feel proud that you tried, whatever the outcome.

This is what life is all about, trying things out to experience the unknown.

Having the opportunity to try new ideas and experiences is a gift that should not be wasted or taken for granted.

We should be eternally grateful that we have the ability and opportunity to experience life.

I am. So should you.

So, what are you going to do? Today, then tomorrow, then the day after that?

Make a positive difference for yourself and the people around you, especially for your kids. Give them the best start possible.

Do you want to be able to look back on your life and say, yup, I tried my best and made a positive difference?

Or will you get to your deathbed with a shed load of regrets, with no time left to make amends.

CHOICE TIME

The **HITS**

Make a positive difference to the world and those around you so that when you are gone, people will remember the good things you did for them and others and say, yup, what a guy.

or

The **SHITS**

Become even more dejected and miserable about life and hate virtually every day, become that grumpy old git that just complains about everything. Achieve nothing worthwhile, and have nothing to be proud of.

Further reading and resources

For further info and study, I would heartily recommend that you check out the following books:

Anxiety and depression

Two rather good books on Anxiety/ depression by Matt Haig:

- Reasons to stay alive
- Notes on a nervous planet

Wellbeing

To help you make the most of life, 2 books from Michael Heppell:

- How to be Brilliant
- Flip it

Philosophy

Philosophy for Life -Jules Evans

Meditations – Marcus Aurelius

Mindset

Mindset – Carol Dweck

Tame that inner Critic – Mike Garde

Health, wellbeing, nutrition & fitness

Thrive – Dean Coulson

Fit, Fuelled and Fired up – David Rogers

Attaining happiness

The Happiness Advantage – Shawn Anchor

Acknowledgements

I have so many people to thank for helping this book become a reality.

Firstly, a big thank you to my wife and kids for their support, patience and encouragement.

Secondly, thank you to my parents, who did a pretty damn good job of bringing me up.

A massive thank you to all my friends who have been there for me over the years and to those of you who have encouraged me to write this book. Especially those who have given their valuable time to provide feedback and support, namely Giulian, Michael, Dominic, Jennifer, David and Ian, very much appreciated.

I would also like to thank my "Write that book" buddies, Jennifer, Maria, Karrie-Ann, Kate, Fiona, Dave and Ian, for their encouragement and support.

Thank you to Michael Heppell, who gave me the push, confidence, and tools to write this book, who helped me believe in myself and also for his encouragement and help to get it published.

Finally, thank you to Mike Garde, who helped remind me why I was writing this book and was instrumental in ensuring it was published.

Printed in Great Britain
by Amazon